Stephanie Stockley was [illegible] With her husband, a manager for the manufacturer Cammel Laird, she travelled all over the world before moving to British Columbia in 1938. The Stockleys lived in Duncan and on Saltspring Island, where they became part of the large English expatriate community in the area at that time. British Columbia has been her home ever since. Much of Stephanie's time has been spent in volunteer work for hospitals and Christ Church Cathedral in Victoria, BC. Besides *Tennis Cow,* she has also published many articles and a volume of verse, *Poems*.

Tennis Cow

a tale of Saltspring Island

Stephanie Stockley

Gregson

First published in 1995 by *Gregson*, an imprint of Gregson Communications Ltd., Victoria, BC.

First edition.

Typeset in Vancouver by The Writing Company.
Printed and bound by Hignell Printers, Winnipeg.

10 9 8 7 6 5 4 3 2 1

Canadian Cataloguing in Publication Data

Stockley, Stephanie, 1901-
Tennis Cow

I. Title
PS8587.T62T46 1994   C813'.54   C94-910618-6
PR9199.3.S86T46 1994

ISBN 0 9698670 0 X

PRINTED AND BOUND IN CANADA

Tennis Cow

This book is dedicated with love to daughter Lois, who started me off fifty years ago before she had to leave me with it on Saltspring Island to enter her own interesting future,

and to daughter Penelope, who in my extreme old age, with mirth encouraged me to revise it.

Chapter One

THE FERRY WAS THREADING its way among the Gulf Islands of the Strait of Georgia, on the Canadian Pacific coast. Caroline Pomfret and her seventeen-year-old daughter, Sophie, who had briefly broken their journey from England to the city of Victoria, were getting near their destination. They stood on deck and gazed through the gathering dusk of a February afternoon at a scene which to Caroline vaguely suggested a Japanese print. Floating in the glass-grey waters they saw many fir-crested, rocky islands. A pair of cormorants skimmed fast away towards a mountain along whose bristly back lay a golden fish of sunset, and the air was soft and damp, beading everything on deck with moisture.

"How very beautiful and silent," murmured Caroline. "I've only seen two houses so far. Do you think, Sophie, the islands can be inhabited?"

"I shouldn't think so, there's probably no water on them. But for camping! What fun to own a little island like that." She pointed to a white crescent of clamshell beach caught up among rocks and trees.

Meanwhile the ferry was taking them up a wide inlet, folded away between hills, on whose timbered slopes they could see clearings, with here and there unpainted wooden houses all of a sudden visible. Some of the slopes had been logged into desolation, bereft. A wharf marked the head of this inlet, where a cove sheltered a cluster of boats. They saw more houses beyond, and a small painted church with a steeple.

The clouds hung down from the mountains. The trees crowded to the water's edge, their shadows pushed in front of them. A bellow split the air, causing Caroline to drop her handbag, which Sophie retrieved. Loose change, English and Canadian, lipsticks, aspirin tablets, and a small cake of soap filched from a hotel bathroom, had tumbled out and were replaced. Sophie was rewarded with a smile.

The ferry engines went into reverse, and shuddering from stem to stern the boat moved on to the end of the wharf. A moment of wet silence enclosed them, and they seemed to float in space; then the deck hand leapt ashore, unwound and lowered the landing apron with which they were then connected. The wash lapped at the wharf, where purple and orange starfish hung in fruity clusters. Sophie noticed with interest the old motor tires hanging as buffers, presumably to protect the spotless paint work of the ferry.

Off went the bus in which the Pomfrets had travelled from Victoria, followed by half-a-dozen cars and a truck. It bumped up the apron, along the wharf, and swished away into the dusk. The two women, carrying their suitcases, followed. They paused uncertainly outside the lit window of a general store. At the same moment an old English car, containing a robust older man and a woman, squealed to a stop.

"You must be the Pomfrets. We are the Noons. Welcome to our island!"

"Yes, here we are," Caroline brightly answered, shaking hands and smiling up at him before turning towards his wife, who was eying them from the car. "Dear Mrs. Noon, how kind of you to meet us." She turned then towards her daughter. "This is, of course, Sophie."

"Welcome after your long journey. My dear Sophie, how much you look like your great-aunt." Mrs. Noon had leaned out to kiss Sophie, who drooped a little. "Your Aunt Mary," she addressed Caroline again, "was such a very old friend, as you must know. So you can understand what a great shock it was when she was taken from us. But we are looking forward to having you. It's too bad that you never met Mary."

"Are you sure that you can bear with us until the house is ready? It's very good of you." Caroline spoke with real gratitude.

"It's an ill wind," the man said, "that blows us *no* good." He gazed with satisfaction at the new arrivals.

"If you mean," said his spouse, looking a little shrill, "If you mean because of poor Mary. . . ."

"Shall we get in?" Caroline suggested quickly, to avert further verbal disaster.

Having tucked them in to the back seat with their bags, Mr. Noon pulled down the ear flaps of his balaclava, and with concentration proceeded to start the car.

"You must call us Jim and Edna," Mrs. Noon cried over

her shoulder, as they lurched out of a large hole in the road and round a bend. "You have always been Carrie and Sophie to us."

"Damn and blast!" muttered the driver.

Sophie took a quick look at her mother's expression and grinned out of the window. No one was in the habit of shortening Caroline's name.

She grinned at the sombre fir trees which climbed in tiers into the darkening sky and said, "That would be nice, Aunt Edna."

Edna began to tell them about the dreadful state of the roads. "It's all politics," she said darkly. "Graft. That's where our taxes go, to line the politicians' pockets. The people around here are mostly CCF and the government won't spend money on their roads. Their own, of course, are different."

"What is CCF?" asked Caroline.

As Edna hesitated, Jimmie took over. "Oh, Communist Canadian Commonwealth Federation," he amended.

"That sounds Conservative enough, James."

"Mrs. Noo-Aunt, Edna," said Sophie, "What is our house like?"

"Arbutus Point? Oh, very nice — though it needs work doing on it. Jimmie has done his best, but there is something a bit haywire with the plumbing. But it's a charming property and, Jimmie says, valuable. . . ."

"I certainly envy you the antiques," Jimmie put in. "Well, here we are, home sweet home."

The car surged through an open gate and stopped before a low, leafy house. A verandah light went on and a slight, grey-haired woman — "James' sister, Rose," said Edna — gave a hand to each of the visitors and saw them in to a warmly lit room, where tea was laid on a table before the glow of logs in an open fireplace.

"It's late for tea, but sherry if you'd rather," Rose said in a pleasant, clear voice. She was quite a bit younger than her brother. "We are so glad you have really come. Arbutus Point needs you. Leave your things in this little room for now. It's Sophie's, but we use it for a cloakroom, too." And she showed them a tiny bedroom near the front door.

Sophie was delighted, and put out a finger to touch a bowl of snowdrops which were admiring themselves in a mirror. "What a sweet room, like a ship's cabin!" She smiled at Rose.

"Electric light!" Caroline was relieved. "Have we got it at Arbutus Point?"

"Yes, just before the war. Mary had it put in, and we at the same time. In fact, she lent us the money to get ours installed." Rose pointed to the stairs which led up to the living room. "The other bedrooms and bath are upstairs — lavatory too, of course, if you would like it."

"It's alright, Rose, there were three nice ones on the boat," said Caroline.

"Three what in a boat?" asked James, barging in through the front door with the suitcases.

"Three men in a boat," Rose answered promptly " — or rather, ladies."

He looked puzzled.

They sat by the fire, and Rose went in to a curtained-off kitchen to make tea. The room was pretty. There were hyacinths in bowls, lots of watercolours on the walls and four different patterned cretonnes on chairs and windows. The couch was clasped, in addition, in a knitted afghan. A number of miniatures and a silhouette hung around the fireplace among some horse brasses, while on the mantlepiece, two Dresden figures flanked a silent carriage clock. Sophie counted seven calendars. The floor was covered in bright blue linoleum. A deerskin lay stiffly before the fire, and a sheepskin in front of the couch. The tea table was clad in a crochet-edged, snowy vestment which took Caroline back to her mother's 'At Home' days.

In a few minutes, Rose returned with a silver teapot, and Edna followed bearing a mountain of buttered potato cakes. On the table already was a rich and smug-looking fruit cake. Edna, who had spent a little time freshening up, appeared much more pleasant without the not-altogether attractive hat she had been wearing. Her hair was fair and faded, and finger-waved. The hyper-thyroid blue eyes were softer. She told them that nearly everything that they used at The Hollies was home-grown or home-made; she made gloves for sale as well. "The firewood," she said, as Jimmie pushed past with an armful of bark and logs, "comes off the beach. Jimmie saws it up."

It was a lovely tea, which Caroline enlivened with a description of life in wartime England. At last she said, "For the rest of my life I should like to live to eat, but unfortunately on Mary's legacy that won't be possible."

"You must become self-supporting, Carrie, as we are," Edna said.

"I will help you all I can," offered James. He was rolling cigarettes on a machine.

Edna docilely licked along the edges of her paper. "I usually lick for the family. One gets to prefer these to tailor-mades. They are better for you and of course, much cheaper, but at first you may find them harder to keep alight."

Tailor-made Canadian cigarettes seemed inexpensive enough to Caroline, and she was already getting used to them. So she thought that, in spite of James, she would go on buying them.

"Mary used to talk about your husband and you for hours," Edna confided as she sat down cosily with Caroline on the couch. "She always hoped that Rupert would bring you out to BC to live. So it was a great blow to her when he was lost in that air-raid. He was more like a son than a nephew. I suppose he was much older than you, so it could really be worse," she added lamely, as a bell rang. "What did actually happen?"

"Oh!" Caroline flinched. She did not feel like explaining Rupert, certainly not to such an audience. Doing his duty as a London air-raid warden, under a flaring, Judas-red sky, he had been killed instantly during one of the early blitzes, when the side of a building fell upon him. It had been a terrible shock. She still carried the trauma of the image, and of the loss.

The bell rang again.

"I am simply longing to hear all about the air-raids at first hand," Edna persisted, "though I suppose they are already out of date now that we have the atomic bomb."

"Mrs. Noon," Sophie broke in, "why do you ignore your telephone when it rings?"

"It hasn't rung, has it?" The pale stare turned on her. Tactful child, thought Rose, now passing the sherry and admiring the flushed young face, framed in straight, pale-lustre hair.

"Isn't that the phone?" Sophie asked, puzzled, as the bell shrilled again.

"Oh yes," James answered, "We are on a party line, you see, which we share with other houses. We all have different rings, ours is two longs and a short. You only hear your own consciously. Oh! Cheerio, happy days and welcome, both of you."

Caroline said, "My God! What a fearful arrangement! I suppose it goes day and night."

"I don't know. Does it?" he grinned at Edna.

"It never bothers me. In fact, I like it," she answered brightly. "It's company."

"Edna listens in," he explained, to her obvious chagrin.

"Are we on this line at Arbutus Point, James?"

"No, I'm afraid you have no telephone at all. I suppose they will soon be available now the war is over. But you can always use ours."

"Then it will take me ages to get *au fait* with your private lives, and," Caroline added, "you with mine."

"Well I feel," Rose added in her comfortable manner, "that as people talk so long, one can hardly get a call in edgeways. You might just as well not have one." She meant, of course, a telephone.

"Do people actually call you Carrie, or Caroline?" Edna suddenly asked.

"The people I'm fond of always call me Caroline," she replied, a shade starchily.

"But such a mouthful," muttered Edna.

A small marmalade cat entered the room at this point and lapped up milk from Jim's saucer.

"My dears, what unlimited butter and milk and cream. I suppose you aren't still rationed for butter?"

"Oh yes, six ounces a week. But we have a little Jersey cow called Mavis, and that makes all the difference. A good little cow — a tennis cow, in fact."

"What's a tennis cow, Mrs. Noon?" Sophie asked gleefully.

"A tennis cow," said Edna, smiling with pleasure at Sophie's reaction, "is an amenable creature found only in BC. Its milking hours adapt themselves to their owners' convenience. For instance, if a last set of tennis is followed by others, our Mavis bears no malice. She'll always wait to be milked until we're finished playing."

"Which reminds me, I'd better go out and do something about her now," said Jim.

"Supper around the fire in about an hour-and- a-half?" suggested Rose, showing Caroline upstairs to her room.

Chapter Two

AROUND EIGHT O'CLOCK that evening, the Pomfrets sat down with the Noons to enjoy bowls of clam chowder. Rose, armed with a storm lantern, had dug the clams out of the beach the night before, when the tide was low. Apparently, there had been lots of Indians down there, too, digging under the bright moon.

"Delicious!" sighed Caroline, accepting another helping. "A kind of Canadian bouillabaisse. How do you make it?"

"I leave the dozen or so clams in a sieve in the stream, to wash the grit out of them. Then I pop the poor things in a pan into a hot oven and try to forget their suffering while they open."

Sophie clicked sympathetically.

"Then I cut off their necks for the cat, make a cream soup with the nectar, add vegetables already cooked — onions, potatoes, and some bits of crisp bacon. Then herbs, the chopped clams too, just before you eat it (but don't boil them, they do go tough) and some cream."

"Do be a lamb and write it all down for me," said Caroline plaintively, "and you, Sophie, can learn to dig them."

The next course was deer steak-and-kidney-pie, flaky of pastry and bubbling with rich brown gravy. The deer meat was a gift from a neighbour, for James no longer went hunting — there was not time. With the pie were home-canned — which seemed to be what the Canadians called bottled, like saying deer-meat for venison — tomatoes, and some potatoes baked in their skins. Both had been Noon-grown. There was milk to drink from Mavis. Sophie started talking to Edna about a small, flat-bottomed boat which she was told lived in the Arbutus Point boathouse. It had been washed ashore a long time ago, in rough weather, and no one had ever claimed it.

"Uncle James says he will caulk and paint her, and show me how it's done. It should be lots of fun, and then I can go fishing."

Edna said nothing to this, but munched angrily, and Sophie, surprised, followed her stare, and saw that James was patting her mother's hand. He was assuring her that he was quite willing to have a shot at the drains if a certain Bill Stokes could be induced to give help. He would have to be called in sooner or later in any case, to mend a leak in the roof. Caroline produced a captivating dimple, and gratefully accepted his offer. Then she asked, "Where does the water come from? We can't be on the main. You are sure there is water?"

"My dear," said Edna, rather nastily, "it's just as well you haven't got to get someone to pump for you. Luckily the water comes down by gravity into a tank."

"As the gentle dew from heaven?"

"Oh no, Caroline, it's piped down from a spring above the house, which flows unceasingly." Edna ladled out huge blackberries, home-canned into the soup bowls which Rose had washed and put back. Then she passed the cream.

"That's alright, then. I'm glad it's not to be another case of Mrs. Porter and her daughter who washed their feet in soda water."

Edna did not smile.

After an interval James remarked that the blackberries grew wild in the Indian reserve and that Rose spent the summer canning fruit, vegetables, chicken, deer-meat and salmon. She had won many prizes at the fairs, and got a great kick out of it. When the meal was finished Sophie and James rose and did the dishes, while Edna telephoned about a meeting, ringing all kinds of numbers and ending each conversation with, "Well, my dear, see you tomorrow at three, then."

Meanwhile, relaxed in the least uncomfortable chair, Caroline lay back with her feet on a stool, and thought how pleasing her legs looked. With a great sigh of cigarette smoke she picked up a copy of *LIFE.* The radio was playing Cesar Franck's *Variations.* In a kind of cupboard behind the kitchen, called the butler's pantry, Rose was now cleaning the greasy sink after James' perfunctory washing up. She twirled the mop between her hands to shake it dry. Sophie finished stacking the clean dishes on shelves in the kitchen, and watched as James put all remnants that were no good for the hens in a red and white container, the lid of which entrancingly clicked open and shut as he pressed a pedal with his foot. After replacing a bowl of flowers on the polished table, James sat down heavily to make more cigarettes for the family. He had milked Mavis and Edna had put the hens to bed.

"I'd like to learn to milk Mavis," Sophie cajoled James, who did not commit himself but looked pleased. When the coffee arrived Rose said "You haven't got into our way yet of drinking tea or coffee with lunch or supper. What is that wonderful music?"

As it came to an end they heard that it was sponsored by Fee Fi Fo's Funeral Parlours. A final complement of chords, as James asked, " Do you know anything about funeral homes?"

"No. I can't say I do. Only that I noticed a great many in Vancouver, very well located. At first I thought they were bars-beverage rooms, beer parlours! What grand names. Whatever do you call spades?"

"Shovels," James loudly answered.

"Anyway, from what I saw of the inside of one beer parlour, I should think the decor is much the same in both. What really puzzled us was a notice in Stanley Park: 'To the comfort stations'. We went in looking for coffee and doughnuts."

"Well," he continued, "just about everyone here is taken to a funeral parlour when they die. And the mortician proceeds to make all the arrangements. They run off your blood, and things like that, and then they inject things. Then they pretty you up in your tuxedo or evening gown, curl your hair or moustache, and make your face up. Then you're ready for display at the Chapel of Chimes, and your family and friends file past, and say, "Oh, how lifelike and peaceful."

"That's quite enough," broke in Edna, "with Mary hardly cold..."

"Oh, Oh!" Caroline moaned, giving way to laughter at the picture of Mary hardly cold, a dread apparition, clad in a frilly blouse, mascara dripping, a rosy bloom.

"I would rather jump in the sea," said Rose. "Or you can be buried at sea. A family across the bay called Rice always are — or is. And the point of land off which they are cast has come to be called Kedgeree Point."

"Rice and fish," added James, labouring the thought.

"Sophie, dear, I think it is time that you filled your mother's hot water bottle," Edna said, studying Caroline's flushed face.

* * * *

"How tactless you are, Mouseykins," Edna had waited till later to scold her husband in what she thought was the privacy of their room.

She was doing her hair up in pipe cleaners. "But for a widow, quite newly bereaved, to laugh at such stories! Could she have been hysterical, do you think?"

"I should say it's a long time since she had a good laugh." James submerged his dentures into a half-filled tumbler. He was scared of forgetting, and leaving them, as was his habit, in the bathroom, where the Pomfrets could hardly fail to see them. Without teeth, in pale blue pajamas of flannelette, and a fluff of hair standing up round his pink head he looked surprisingly infantile. He glanced at Edna and then away again, thinking that in her pipe cleaners she looked a bit like Medusa.

At the same time, the hysterical widow was lubricating her face from an exciting new jar of American beauty cream. She got into bed and dreamed not about caskets but about Rupert in his element striding around a celestial golf course. Sophie, cuddling her hot water bottle, was reading, in an old copy of *The Countryman*, an article by a professional islander. "If only Aunt Mary had owned an uninhabited island," she murmured.

Chapter 3

SOPHIE YAWNED. SHE HAD GOT UP EARLY and found her way down to the beach by a path that followed the fence of Mavis' pasture, where she noticed familiar bracken crooks already beginning to force up through the ground. The tide had been low, the sea unbreaking and with an oily sheen like that of the pussy willows which she had found growing beside a stream. A backdrop of slate-coloured mountains and dove-grey islands hung from a slightly luminous sky. The beach looked muddy. Driftwood lay about and was waist-high above high tide mark, where alder and willow, maple and cedar hung their live branches over a cemetery of castaway logs. There were huge carcasses of Douglas fir and cedar. Many were bleached or pitted with barnacles, and riddled with toredo worm. Some were newly washed ashore from a shattered log boom. Every rock below tide mark was rough and jagged with barnacles. As Sophie walked down towards the sea, everywhere she saw large white shells, empty. Squirts of water shot up from holes in the mud, making her legs wet and puzzling her considerably. She stood there watching black and white diving ducks, and gulls who dropped swiftly into the still water. Only the gulls broke the enormous silence with their occasional mewings, and some kind of fish rose and plopped back.

Soon she turned reluctantly homeward, to help Rose get breakfast, and take her mother an early cup of tea. While arranging the pussy willow stems she had picked, she could hear Edna's voice buzzing like a bluebottle behind the raspberry canes, talking alternatively to the hens and to Jimmie, as he furbished up Spork and Spam, the two young pigs who lived in a rustic dwelling at the far end of the garden. Round the kitchen curtain came Rose, wearing a peasant apron over slacks, and adjusting horn-rimmed spectacles with floury fingers. "The worst of these things is that they will slip down," she complained. "I wanted pince-nez again, but Jim has a theory that it's better to have unnatural looking glasses than the sort that blend with your face. He says its more chic." She grinned, suddenly looking, for all the world, twelve years old. "I keep meaning to put some adhesive tape on them. What do you like in sandwiches, Sophie? Cheese and our own pickled walnuts, cold bacon and lettuce, or peanut butter and jelly?"

"I've never had peanut butter."

Rose brought her a spoonful.

"Oh, peanut butter, please!" and she licked the spoon. "Rose, could I take a bottle of milk? Skim would do. It's too marvelous to be able to drink milk again."

"My dear, of course. You shall be able to bathe in skim milk if you like. Before the animals get at it. How lovely that willow looks. Come and help with the sandwiches," she went on, affectionately, taking Sophie by the arm.

Caroline, slouched down in a chair, was examining the kitchen stove. "Look, Sophie, isn't this ingenious? You fill this" — and she pointed to a chromium-plated hopper attached to the side of the cooker — "about three times a day. The little door at the bottom is the draught. The sawdust goes on and on slipping down into the side of the stove as it burns. Rose fills it last thing at night, shuts it down, and it's still burning in the morning. The house is warm."

"I know it is," murmured Sophie.

"The sawdust comes from a mill and they store it in their shed." As she spoke, there was a muffled explosion. A puff of smoke and tiny sparks burst out of the draught door.

"Good heavens! Is it meant to do that?"

"Oh yes," said Rose reassuringly. "It never seems to amount to anything, not even to singe a cat. A back-draught, Jim calls it."

Rose then told them how she rubbed the inside of the hopper now and again with emery paper, so that the sawdust would not stick, and how, in the summer, she sprinkled on water to make it burn more slowly.

Half an hour later James took the Pomfrets off in the car, to show them Arbutus Point. Shafts of pale sunlight now filtered through the enormous Douglas firs onto the road. A moss-covered snake fence zig-zagged beside them, deep among polished salal bushes and a mess of brambles.

"Oh James, do let's stop before long," implored Caroline. He drew up at once, as they reached a clearing. Down below, tranquil, shining, lay the unexpected inlet, and the distant mountains, almost dissolved violet in the soft air, rose like a wall. Groups of arbutus trees stood, saffron, auburn, olive, their peeling bark smocked back upon satin-smooth trunks. Their stiff, enamelled leaves flashed back the sunlight. Caroline exclaimed, "Madrona!" with a perfectly splendid Spanish accent, as she and Sophie got out of the car.

"Arbutus, arbutus, isn't it, Uncle James?" Sophie was over the fence and uncurling a paper-thin piece of bark, pretending to smoke an arbutus bark cigar.

"Well, Sophie, arbutus is what it's called here. But in the States they do say madrona." He smiled at her fairness among the red tree trunks. "Arbutus Point is nice, I think. Rose says that it's a pity a jollier name wasn't found for the dogwood tree. That really is a picture when the big white blossoms come out. Only a month or two now." A bird with a long tail and reddish breast distracted him. "A towhee," he pointed out.

"Why don't any of your birds sing?" Sophie had already noticed the hush that hung over woods even in February, the mating month. Jim gave Caroline and himself cigarettes while he thought about this.

" 'And no birds sing,' " prompted Caroline.

"It's due to the Gulf stream that you get all those singing birds in England, on migration."

"But you have the Japanese current here," Sophie suggested.

"The flowering currant? It's not out yet."

"Oh come on!" Caroline laughed, and led them back to the car. James was now wishing that, despite the somewhat better weather, he had worn the balaclava. Hardness of hearing was some protection from these intelligent women.

They immediately drove past the boundary fence between the Noon place and the Pomfret's, and continued in silence until they came to a turning in the bush, marked by a metal mailbox which swivelled on top of a post, and which bore the name 'Pomfret' on its side. Outgoing mail was collected from this three days a week before midday, and incoming mail delivered the same days, Jim now explained, and one could safely leave money for stamps inside it.

"I wish I could afford a car," Caroline groaned. They turned over the cattle guard into their private road to Beaver Point and were under the shade of the firs, the cones of which carpeted the drive. They paused at a clearing by a pond, where a pair of mallards was swimming among rushes. They drove then through an orchard of very old, gnarled trees, many of them 500 years old, James informed them, and Sophie got out to open a gate in the picket fence, allowing James to drive into the grassy yard.

There was a house, built of local cedar, painted white. It had a porch over a well-proportioned front door with a fan light and a brass knocker. The windows wore faded green shutters, and the sound and smell of the sea was strong. Snowdrops grew by the fence.

"Oh what fun!" exclaimed Sophie, as her mother performed the ceremony of opening the door with the key

James gave her. There was a tussle before she could throw it back, and they all went in.

"It smells good," Caroline breathed thankfully.

"We've been down here every week to light a fire, but it does need airing. The electric and water are turned off, and the pipes drained, though you're too near the sea to get frost. By the way, Caroline, the lawyer came last week to take the inventory." He started to lead them across the hall, quoting what he had often heard Mary Pomfret say to her guests. "The house is built on different levels. Bedrooms and bathroom on this floor." Caroline paused to admire a fine grandfather clock which stared back dumbly. A flight of stairs curved downwards to the right. "Below is the kitchen and living room, isn't that quaint? It takes advantage of the view," he continued to quote, but the Pomfrets hardly waited to hear him. They were already headed downstairs, exclaiming with delight from the window half-way. James, sighing a little, began to wind up the grandfather clock.

The stairs led straight into a long white room, walls and ceiling awash with light reflected from the sea, which nearly encompassed the rocky point. Half-burned logs behind a fire guard appeared forlorn on the open fireplace whose knobbly granite stones looked hard to please.

"The view is superb," called Caroline, from one of the three long windows, where she stood framed against a satin-striped sea. Sophie thought she would have liked a painting of her mother against that background, with her mermaid look, and her arbutus bark hair. The rocky point at which they were looking was turf-covered on one side, and on the other sloped gently to a white-speckled clamshell beach, littered with driftwood and kelp. Right and left were the auburn trees.

In a shiver of light they moved about the big room, examining the furniture, while James was seeing to the furnace in the basement. "Solid but good," Caroline remarked, "one or two quite valuable pieces. But, blast it, we're not allowed to sell the furniture! And now it's all been appraised, so we're stuck with it."

Aunt Mary had left in her will five hundred dollars a year to Caroline, together with Arbutus Point and its contents on this condition, that she should bring Sophie out to live there. At the end of three years, they were free to keep or sell the property and its contents. But the income would continue in perpetuity. Caroline accepted the bequest with some reluctance. But her wartime job in censorship had ended, and she found herself tired. Sophie, on the other hand, was delighted. Their small capital, which they were allowed to bring out, might just keep them together with the legacy.

"Mother, those mountains are in the United States — about eighty miles away Uncle James thinks."

"How thrilling, Sophie. Now let's take a proper look at the kitchen."

Through the doorway to the right of the living room fireplace, James had already lit an oil-burning range in the dim, cold kitchen, and a kettle was coming to boil.

"You don't know how lucky you are," he greeted them. "Mary scrapped the wood-burning stove just before the war and we all have the electric, too. You fill this thing from the barrels of oil in the outside shed. That's the breakfast nook," and he nodded towards the bay window where green-painted settles, with cushions, were built in on either side of the drop-leaf table. "This clamshell is an ashtray off your very own beach. Edna paints pictures in them with oils for bazaars. And this is an ingenious thing which I never saw in the old country."

He lowered on its hinges from an embrasure in the wall a padded ironing board.

"That reminds me," said Caroline, "does the laundry call?"

"Mary and her companion used to do it all at home. There isn't even a washing machine. No place here to send it to." He wandered out the back door to get their sandwiches from the car.

Caroline glanced uneasily at her daughter. "How extraordinary. There will be a lot to do, without a servant. But perhaps we could find an evacuee who wants to stay on, or an inexpensive Indian. Or even a paying guest. Meanwhile, we'd better be careful to keep friends with James — he's so domesticated. A pity Mary's companion went back home."

"Mother, you're awful. Wasn't he sweet about the breakfast nook?"

"All nods and becks and wreathed smiles. Do you think he would come in once a week to do the ironing? He seems to love that board so. I overheard Edna call him 'Mouseykins' the other night. She's only allowed to do it in private, I expect. If I blackmail them, maybe she will lend him to us."

Chapter 4

ON SATURDAY, THE CHIEF shopping day of the week, James was to take the Pomfrets to Ganges. He was busy filling the trunk of the car with boxes and eggs, to leave at the creamery. Someone had to stay home because there would be no room in the car on its return, loaded with sacks of feed and family provisions. Rose had insisted that she had to stay and get tea ready for the Sunlight Sewing Circle at four o'clock. "Even though it's just tea and doughnuts, I do have other things to do."

She looked rather sweet standing there, with the wind flipping her prematurely grey hair and her neatly tailored slacks, and with her nice teeth all showing.

"I wish they'd let me stay behind and help her," thought Sophie, "I bet she's going off fishing, or digging clams, or on some funny adventure. She lives a life of her own."

"Blue to match your eyes." Jim was peering from Sophie's tweed coat to her face, and back again. There was no reply to that kind of remark, so she smiled dutifully. Just then Edna hurried from the house. She wore a woolly mauve ensemble under a macintosh, and trailed sprays of winter jasmine for the church. Caroline, trim in grey tweeds, was already sitting in the front seat. Edna, with a sour look, climbed in beside Sophie, and they set off. They crossed the bridge above Fulford Harbour, which they had passed on the day of their arrival, and could see the ferry, ready for her labours at the government wharf. She was an unreal-looking craft, more like a painted toy which children might drag around the garden.

Yachts and fishing boats were also lying in the perfect anchorage of the cove, and the hulls of a couple under construction hung in slipways. Now their route led in a different direction, north, through a valley overshadowed with the smears of logged-off mountains, blackened snags everywhere, and poor, derelict young trees torn sideways by the ruthless, high-lead logging methods. Caroline was impelled to ask if there had been a fire, which gave Jim the chance to explain.

"The logging companies have to burn the slash each fall, otherwise it might cause a fire hazard. That burns away the thin soil on the rocks, so nothing will grow there for ages. Of course, the companies are beginning to replant."

"But so wasteful and untidy," Caroline said. "This must be the most wasteful and untidy country anywhere. Nothing but snags and tin cans and endless awful shacks."

They were now crossing another wooden bridge, over mudflats.

"All those 'awful' shacks belong to the Indians — this is the reserve." Edna pointed to the bank of the inlet, where unpainted wood cabins seemed to grow out of the mud. Outside many stood handsome cars which could not be repossessed for debt, as Jimmie explained. There were also sheep and chickens.

On the fences of the reserve, clots of wool were hanging out to dry, before they were spun to knit the native socks and sweaters. Sophie waved to a small child balanced on the top rail of the bridge, his plump olive face and gently slanting eyes making him look like pictures she had seen of Eskimo children.

"We would like to tear all this down," Edna said, "and make a decent approach to the town. The Indians have all the best land, and just look what they do with it. You wait till you hear the noise they make with their dances, their potlatches. They're not supposed to buy or drink alcohol, of course," and she sniffed. But Rose yesterday had remarked that quite a lot of Indians joined up and went overseas to risk their lives in the War, so Sophie thought they must feel their rather sad-looking reservation was worth fighting for; and the potlatches Rose had described sounded complicated and rather awe-inspiring. Edna's tone made her feel sick but felt she must hold her tongue. Why did the Indians live in such poverty? She had better ask Rose. There was so much to understand.

'Welcome to Ganges!' flaunted itself across the road on a banner, while hoardings were inviting them to eat at Cecil's Place or visit Joe's Tire Hospital.

"This is the real approach to town," said James with a grin, and started to look for a parking place. They fitted themselves into an awkward corner of a sort of square, sloping down to the wharf.

A large, wood-built store, with a false front partially hiding a tin roof, took up most of one side, with Cecil's cafe next to it. On the other side were oil storage tanks among trees and rocks. A few houses looked out over the water from a jutting promontory. A tall man detached himself from a group of people standing outside the store, in response to James' cry of "Hullo, 'ullo, 'ullo, come and meet the new arrivals!" He was introduced as Ambrose Mallow.

"And how was the Old Country when you left it? Pretty short of rations, eh? That comes of electing a Labour government. Though, as a matter of fact, there isn't much to eat here, either. It comes and goes — no lard, no toilet paper to be had today, but ice cream at Cecil's, so come and have some." He called the cafe "Ceecil's."

"Isn't it rather early for ice cream? Now a nice cup of coffee. . . ." Caroline smiled tentatively, and was surprised to hear him give a little groan. She followed his glance to see a boy scout with a white beard, dismounting from a bicycle onto the wooden sidewalk.

"Sir Ernest, Sir Ernest!" Edna cried, "Here is Mary's niece, Mrs. Pomfret, and her little daughter, Sophie. Sir Ernest Boyce, dear."

"Oh indeed? This is a great pleasure. Welcome to the island. You have been anxiously awaited since Miss Pomfret's untimely death. A wonderful woman, Mary Pomfret, and a great gardener. Her antirrhinums have been blooming to a nicety since the week she died. I am just on my way to the scout hall, you wouldn't care to come, Miss Sophie? It would be so jolly if you would take over my Cubs. Your aunt was the Brown Owl, you know. And perhaps one day, you, Miss Pomfret, might be able to give the scouts a little talk on the subject of heroism in shelters, heroism indeed, indeed! I expect you are going to refresh yourselves at Cecil's."

"Well, perhaps later," Caroline murmured doubtfully, "but I'm sure my daughter would love to become involved with the Cubs."

"My wife and I will be coming around in our boat to call, just as soon as the weather becomes more clement. But now I must fly, as I am taking the boys off to look for Indian arrowheads, of which we have a fine collection."

"Mother!" Sophie gasped as he turned his back. "How dare you!"

"Come on Edna. For God's sake, let's get going," said Mallow, and all of them trooped into the cafe and sat in a booth."

"Coffee please," said Caroline.

"Yes indeed, my dear Mrs. Pomfret. Or even a Coca Cola, if you prefer."

Mallow combed an imaginary beard through his fingers. "Lord, what an old cuttlefish!"

Two large young men, obviously twins, emerged from a further booth, and, passing, smote James and Mallow with "Hiya!" They were clad in lumber jackets of red, green and black check, and carried posies of double ice cream cones.

"Not working today?" James asked, after he had introduced them as the Stanway twins, logger sons of the vicar.

"Sure we're working, but we had to bring a man down to hospital. He's not hurt too bad, they figure he's just bruised. A log rolled on him." They appeared to speak in turn.

"I don't know how your mother has a moment's peace, with you two working in the woods. It's worse than the war," Edna said.

"Jeepers, yes, Mrs. Noon," they agreed, sadly.

When they had gone, smiling over their shoulders at Sophie, Caroline unbelievingly asked James, "Did you say the Vicar's sons?"

"Yes. Fine lads. They were overseas with the RCAF."

The ice cream and coffee had arrived, and as James and Sophie went to put a nickel in the jukebox, Mallow asked Caroline what she thought of the place, while lighting her cigarette.

"Very high-class," she smiled, "but I'm bewildered."

"Mrs. Pomfret," he said seriously, "you will learn in time, if you stay, not to be surprised at the jobs people do. Believe me, it's the finest things happen in this country, and the ones you miss most when you go home. The right attitude to a job of work. Do you know, Moya, my wife, has just bought a washing machine from the proceeds of her second-hand clothes dealings? And I, a respectable remittance man, often help out by working on the roads. Jim here works off his taxes digging ditches along his stretch of the road. This won't prevent you all coming back to eat bread and cheese with us when you've finished your shopping, I do hope?

The old woman would love to see you. We can give Rose a tinkle to explain."

When they finally rose, Edna gave the wilting jasmine to Sophie to take around the corner to the church. Mrs. Stanway would be doing the flowers there, and would be most grateful. Then she and Caroline went off to do the shopping.

In Banbury's, the general store and post office, Edna produced a list, while Caroline investigated these new surroundings with mild curiosity. She fingered the heavy material and white wool of the Indian sweaters, with their patterns of totem birds and beasts, hand-knitted, black and brownish. Both Jim and Mallow had been wearing such sweaters. They cost quite lot, fifteen to twenty-five dollars, but were attractive and practical, shed water and were warm and she wished she could afford one.

The shoe department was uninviting, full of toeless female footwear, high heels with no backs, rubber overshoes, and some more practical "gum boots." She visited a counter laden with men's work garments, yellow and blue shiny sateen jackets, labelled windbreakers, mackinaws in festive checks, great, grey, itchy looking work socks, and piles of rigid blue jeans. Edna kept bringing over people for her to meet whom Caroline knew she would fail to recognize again. They nearly all said, "Well, how do you find the island, Mrs. Pomfret?" And she nearly always answered, "Oh, enchanting," though this was not strictly true.

"What is that stuff you're buying?" she asked Edna, intrigued by the gleaming, damp white mass.

"This? Cottage cheese. It's all they have today, no cheddar. We usually make it at home. You would call it curds. Two pounds of hamburger, please." The assistant dug into a scarlet mass this time.

"Can that be mince?" muttered Caroline, somewhat disappointed after hearing the exotic name.

"Hamburger is wonderful. Rose makes it into almost everything."

"I suppose she makes no bones about it," Caroline was appalled to hear herself answer. She must indeed be reduced to a low ebb.

When she moved away again, she overheard Edna ask in a very low voice for chocolate bars, and turned to see her receive two from under the counter, pay for them and start to eat.

Later on, when Edna had gone to a different counter, Caroline tried the same thing, and was given a bar with peanuts in it, which she too devoured. Then she went outside, and James was there to carry the groceries to the car, already loaded with animal feed.

"Where's Sophie?" her voice came out thick with chocolate peanuts.

"She took the flowers to the church," Edna said, swallowing hard, and staring suspiciously. Gluttonous pig, thought Caroline. She walked over to give Sophie a call, and going through the well-kept churchyard, heard her voice on the porch.

"But don't you think," Sophie was asking eagerly, "that Joad changes all one's abstract values?"

A man's laugh answered, "I was at school with Joad. Perhaps that's why I don't."

"Is this your mother, by any chance?" Mr. Stanway was large and pink and unbuttoned looking. His smile was shy and pleasant, and he and Sophie seemed already to have reached an understanding. He now told Caroline that his wife was at home with a cold, and that Sophie had kindly offered to do the flowers, while he pruned rose trees in the churchyard. But he and his wife would be looking forward to going out to Arbutus Point when the Pomfrets were properly installed. Caroline appeared charmed, and said that she was glad that Sophie had been a good child and talking of children, didn't he lay claim to that splendid pair of twins dressed up as loggers?

"Peter and Mark? Could you understand a word of their strange lingo? I confess I find it hard to follow. They're native sons, you know. Mrs. Pomfret, I do hope that you and Sophie will be happy here. This is a very tranquil and healing existence that we islanders live."

Chapter 5

THE AMBROSE MALLOWS' HOUSE was old and brown, and built, of course, of wood. It rambled up the rocks that overlooked the harbour of Ganges. Leaving their car, the Noons and Pomfrets climbed a path among rockeries which Edna stated would soon be a veritable fairyland. At the top, a woman in navy slacks and fisherman's jersey left off weeding a bed of aconites and, removing gardening gloves, came to meet them. She had a dark, grave face, big grey eyes, and crisp black hair.

"How very nice of you to come," she welcomed the Pomfrets. "Edna, how well you look, and you too, James."

"A little tired," Edna sighed.

They went up a few more steps into the hall, and through that to a pleasantly untidy room, with its windows framing the magnificent view down the harbour. Two spaniels moved politely from the window seat to make friends. They were rather fat. Mrs. Mallow said their names were Bracken and Fern. She waved a pack of cigarettes around, remarking that soup and sandwiches were ready in the kitchen anytime. Ambrose had acquired ice, and was mixing drinks.

"Yes, Moya, I'm really very well on the whole," Edna contrived after an interval of thought. "Wonderful what a chiropractor can do. I only wish that Rose would go to him, she has sciatica." She turned to Caroline, who responded that she wasn't surprised. Sophie, meanwhile, sniffed at a beer mug frothing with jonquils, and then sat down with the dogs on the hearth rug. The door bumped open, Mallow entered with a loaded tray.

"They are too fat, I know," his wife said to Sophie, who was crooning over the pair. "All the exercise they get is going out fishing with me in the boat. Though they do sometimes go off on their own, they miss the hunting."

"Yes, indeed, no time for hunting now, with all the housekeeping to do. My poor wife is delicate, alas. She has to be careful, she's approaching a critical time in a woman's life. You know what I mean, Edna," he winked.

"Been sampling the drinks," his wife asserted.

"Those dogs," he continued, "live on a staple diet of fish. They have an ancient and fish-like smell, don't you think, Sophie?"

"They smell heavenly, just like bracken and fern. Do you get many fish here, Mrs. Mallow?"

"Lots of rock cod, cod, and later on, salmon. There are crabs at Fernwood, you know."

"If we can catch fish off Arbutus Point," Caroline mused, "that will help. Fish and eggs. Cottage cheese, and lots of milk and butter when we get the cow. And fruit and vegetables."

"A cow, Mother?" Sophie called, aghast. "But who will milk it?"

"It would have to adapt itself to James' visits until we learn how. Yes, Edna. A tennis cow."

"I've lived out here for fifteen years," Moya said in a low voice to Caroline, "and people still tell me at parties about their bloody tennis cow."

"Oh yes," Mallow agreed, "and when we come to visit you at Arbutus Point, which we mean to do frequently, we shall always draw your attention to a certain island opposite and say, "That is the island on which they put the Doukhobors," and after a time it will become one of your own cherished observations. You will answer, "Ambrose, my dear, there is just time before dinner for you to see the island where they put the Doukhobors," and we will stroll down arm in arm towards the sunset."

"Well, why did they?" Caroline asked.

"As a protest against the forced education of their children, the Doukhobor mammas would appear on the streets stark naked. At last the authorities had the whole lot removed to this uninhabited island. They had, of course, also been practicing incendiarism on public buildings. But all they really wanted was to be left alone."

They finished their drinks and moved into the comfortable kitchen, where they settled around the table and ate sandwiches, cheese and fruit.

"Cheese!" James said accusingly. "You've been black-marketing, Mallow."

"Blackmailing more likely," said Moya. "But remember, we don't get unlimited butter like you. In fact, there isn't any butter in the house, we had to use margarine for the sandwiches. Please tell us about England, Mrs. Pomfret. I haven't been back since '37. I suppose, after all their heroic experiences, people at home will have nothing in common with us. One is utterly out of touch."

"It wasn't our fault that the Japs didn't invade BC," said her husband, rolling his eyes piously upward. "One of their submarines did shell a lighthouse on the west coast."

"And what about the incendiary balloons that they sent over to burn our forests? And the mines they laid in the St. Lawrence? And the Aleutian Island campaign?"

"Not the Japs in the St. Lawrence, surely?" said Caroline.

"The enemy," Edna summarized, "East and West. With our first line of retreat the Rockies."

"I wish that I'd had the capital or the initiative to buy property on the coast then," said Mallow. "When the Jap scare was on, many of our friends departed for the Okanagan or Banff, and their places were up for sale at ridiculously low prices. One couldn't have gone wrong, because if there had been an invasion one would have lost everything anyway. And if there wasn't, one would have made a fortune. Though you couldn't foretell the boom in property that's happened since, of course."

Moya said bitterly, "It's been a wonderful war for Canadians, except for those who went over, and their families."

As Caroline started to talk about wartime England, Sophie admired her light touches, and the deeper feeling. She wished she was more like her, but perhaps Edna was right and she was a throwback to Aunt Mary, and would prefer to spend her life on this strange island, a mixture of suburban and primeval. She was beginning to think so.

"A penny for your thoughts," James hissed in her ear, making her jerk half her coffee onto the table cloth. She gave him a reproachful look before she turned in speechless misery to Moya, who calmly covered the spreading stain with a dish of fruit.

"Not important," she reassured with her rare smile, "one just pops it into the new washing machine."

James sheepishly asked if Moya had indeed bought this machine with her ill-gotten gains from the shop.

"I'll say," responded her husband, "and I believe she's planning for me to take in the neighbour's laundry now."

"My dear, I haven't exactly bought it, only put a few payments down. But as I hope to sell Edna a fur coat directly, it will be you, James, who must pay the next few installments."

The women went to visit the shop, up a steep little scarlet-painted staircase, in a large attic bedroom hung with racks of clothes. Sophie and Caroline looked first at the view. They could see a CPR freighter, white, yellow and black, heading up among the islands over the bluebell sea, which was criss-crossed with boom logs. At regular intervals loaded logging trucks appeared at the road edge. One by one, the huge logs toppled off sideways, and in a cascade of spray rolled into the booming ground below. Then they were ridden and pushed into place by men whose skill was fascinating to watch, as they leapt or strode from log to bobbing log, which rolled and slithered under their caulked boots. Meanwhile, in the room behind, Edna was squeaking with joy over a mauve satin bed jacket. "Just the thing for early morning tea, or breakfast in bed. How much?"

"Two dollars."

"James always liked me in mauve."

"I would have thought your best colour would be grey," remarked Caroline, casually pulling on a smart suede cap. "That's nice," she said, looking in the long mirror. "I hope I won't catch anything."

"I can vouch for everything, Modom. Most of the things come from people I know — some from Seattle, and some from Vancouver and Victoria, via the cleaners. And all the rest via the washing machine. That model will be a dollar to you."

"I'll give you seventy-five cents — cash."

"It's a deal. Shall I wrap it up or will you wear it?"

"Wear it, please," said Caroline as she counted out the money, looking carefully at the nickels, with which she was not quite yet familiar. "I never can remember what two-bits is."

"Twenty-five cents," Moya kindly elucidated, and then asked if she could sell any clothes Caroline got tired of. "I have to charge ten per cent commission, as my standard of living is rising so."

"Goodness only knows that the wardrobe in the new house is bursting with Aunt Mary's garments. But I would want some for private bundles for Britain, and some we can convert ourselves. But the rest — 'moth and dust doth destroy.' "

"Moth and dust? Moth and rust!" corrected Edna. "And if you are thinking of selling that beautiful purple silk dressing gown, please let me know, as I should be glad to buy it if it is within my means, though Mary did once say something about giving it to me."

"My dear Edna, I know the one, and of course you shall have it as a very slight return for all your kindness, and anything else that is of any good to you."

There was warmth in Caroline's voice, and she was rewarded by seeing Edna's face light up.

"Hoy!" roared a voice up the stairs, "What about your meeting, Edna?" Edna wriggled out of a well-worn musquash, crying, "We must fly," seized her bed jacket, and hurried down the stairs.

"Why don't you and Sophie stay for tea?" Moya said quickly. "Timothy Spens, who I expect you've heard of, is coming round in his boat, and he would enjoy taking you back. He lives aboard her in Fulford Harbour. I think he'll interest you, and I haven't heard nearly enough about your trip yet."

* * * *

"There is *Woodwind*, coming into the wharf," Mallow later remarked, passing the glasses to Sophie.

"Oh good," said Moya. "Tim is rather amusing, you know. He's a nephew of the Bryces, and has just come to

BC again, after spending most of the war in the Censorship in Bermuda. The navy took over *Woodwind* for patrol work, but she's been refitted, and is as good as new. Tim is rather a poseur perhaps, but definitely intelligent. And you'll have your censorship work in common, if nothing else."

They had started tea when Spens came in. "How wise of me to follow my homing instinct," he said, dropping a kiss on top of Moya's head, but glancing at Caroline with queer, light-green eyes.

"What a heavenly boat, Mr. Spens," said Sophie. "I watched you coming in through the glasses."

"*Woodwind*? Yes, she's a grand boat. You must come on board. How nice to meet you at last."

"What about taking Mrs. Pomfret and Sophie home to the Noons in her?" asked Mallow.

"But of course, I would love to. And then Rose will ask me to stay for supper. I've invented a new cocktail, 'Sea Cow Cream', which we'll try on the way round."

"Well, if you're sure it's no bother. . . ." And for another half hour they talked happily.

Spens and Pomfrets then said goodbye, and went down by a shortcut, through the garden and by the churchyard to the Yacht Club, where the lovely *Woodwind* was tied up. She was white, gleaming with fresh paint, forty feet in length, with a six cylinder gas engine. She had been built locally, Spens told them, at Graham's Yard in Fulford Harbour, two years before the war, and was a fine sea boat.

"I've dreamed of a boat like this all my life," Sophie said with rapture. Spens was charmed, and smiled over this nice maiden's head at Caroline, who was staring at him thoughtfully. "I can't have met you before can I?" she asked, as they went aboard.

"If so, how could I have forgotten?"

They went into the roomy cockpit, furnished with seats, a drop leaf table and an icebox. A double bunk cabin came next, then a tiny galley and a washroom, both splendidly equipped. There were lockers and a built-in bookcase, and electrically lit old brass bulkhead lamps. Up in the wheelhouse, forward, was a neatly made bunk, where Spens told them he slept. Caroline was pleased, and Sophie more than ever enraptured, as she studied the glass-covered charts.

"Do you mind if we mix that drink before we start?" he asked. "Would you help me, Sophie?" and Caroline was left in the wheelhouse with her thoughts.

Their having drunk a preliminary cocktail, with Sophie's rather on the small side, Spens showed her how to untie the boat and then coiled the lines on deck. He started the engine and they slid out into the harbour, with pearly water and oyster shell evening all about them. It took only a short time to go round to the Noon's anchorage, but long enough for the moon to lift above the fir trees, and Timothy, as he had now become, rowed them ashore one at a time in the pram, which he lifted up onto the driftwood.

"Bleached cedar by moonlight, or ravaged bones of the sea cows?" he mused, peering at the dim sea wrack.

In retaliation Caroline quoted Eliot, " 'Under a juniper tree their bones sang scattered and shining.' "

"Yoohooo!" creaked James' voice from somewhere above them. He was calling Mavis in to the accompaniment of bangs on the milking pail. As they climbed the clamshell path in silence, following the fence to the garden, Sophie saw the little house with affection, its welcoming lights streaming from the windows. She sniffed the cold smell of wet moss and heard the tree frogs croak. Through the glass of the verandah door she could see Edna, seated at the piano, and faintly the tinkle of the Kerry Dancers came out to them.

Chapter 6

IN THE NIGHT, CAROLINE AWOKE, hearing the wind and the waves, and remembered where she was and felt desperately homesick. But when she woke again to the morning light and gentle clatter of Rose among the breakfast dishes below, she was again almost at home. No doubt she and Sophie would shortly be as comfortable in British Columbia as any of the expatriates they had already encountered, and who one could not honestly imagine ever settling back in the Old Country again. She smiled at the thought, and cheerfully dressed herself. After several weeks at the Noons, the thought of moving to her own house was delightful. And now that the trunks had at last arrived, and had been delivered to Arbutus Point, and the few odd jobs which needed doing there were done, they were to move in today.

After breakfast, Spens arrived, and took them both, together with the Noons, around in his boat. The furnace was lit, the house warm and they all started to unpack the trunks in the living room.

"Take care of those horses!" Caroline said, as Spens unwrapped two curiously shaped packets. "Please take them upstairs, and put them on my chest looking out of the window. They are my dearest possessions."

He went obediently up to the floor above, carrying the small pair of ancient Chinese horses. Caroline, meanwhile, fearing she might be going to sneeze, and she always did when there was anything like this going on, went outside by the back door to get some fresh air and pick a rain-sparkling bunch of snowdrops, growing among the daffodil shoots she saw all about her.

In the living room Sophie was trying to prevent Rose from doing all the work. "This is your day off," she said. "You're not to unpack." But Rose was enjoying herself too much to stop. To her it was like Christmas. Sophie went up with an armful of possessions, just as Caroline came back with the snow drops, and came back down, laughing. "What do you think? Tim is curled up under your eiderdown, reading *Strewelpeter*. He's almost asleep, and he's rearranged the entire room. It looks wonderful." She was carrying a box of Rogers' Chocolates, which she had been carefully saving for this day. "Edna, do have a chocolate."

"May I take two? My idea of bliss is to eat a hard and a soft one together. You see, we hardly ever had candies at the Vicarage when I was a child. These are so good!"

"Of course you can," said Sophie warmly.

"Attaboy!" James helped himself and passed the box to Rose. Caroline remarked, with her mouth full, how all her chocolates used to have nibbles in them — made by a small Sophie in search of the perfect sweet. "I remember, Mama, and it took me ages to settle on peppermint creams. Orange and chocolate cream I never did like."

After a while Tim reappeared, looking rested. He looked at the nearly empty box reproachfully. "You are all doing your best to spoil your appetites for my lunch." Seizing the box, he went off to the kitchen to prepare his famous omelettes, which needed a clutch of Edna's eggs.

The rest of the unpacking was quickly finished, the trunks stowed in the basement, and they went to enjoy his cooking efforts. Afterwards, he turned to Edna. "Your turn to do the dishes. James has got the water scalding hot." Rose protested, but was dragged off with the others, down to the boathouse, to examine Sophie's dinghy, which was brown, rather shabby, and in need of caulking. James said that he would see to it if Spens lent him some caulking tools. Paint he had.

"But not this time, James," said Spens, "I'll do it myself, while Sophie reads aloud. What are you going to call her, Sophie?"

" 'Gull' is a pretty name," Rose suggested. "But isn't she too flat-bottomed and duck-like?"

"How about 'Poppet?' " Spens put in.

"No, 'Moppet'," said Caroline firmly, and that was her name.

"Yes, I like it." Sophie sounded surprised.

James, meanwhile, said nothing. His face was quite red and he looked cross. "It looks as if you're planning to stay on here, then?" he now addressed Spens.

"I'll be in and out for a bit, to keep an eye on things."

" 'Oh, fat white woman whom nobody loves,' " mused Caroline, half aware that Edna was walking down the path towards them, well wrapped in the musquash she had finally bought from Moya, and wearing a pair of nice, home-built, wash-leather gloves. James had gone off huffily to meet her.

"Why do you walk through the fields in gloves?" wondered Spens.

"I'm ready," called Edna. "The kitchen is all neat and tidy, Caroline, ready for you to begin your new life. We must be getting back."

So they embarked, leaving the two Pomfrets gazing after them, turning away at last, a little embarrassed, to take up their new life. Spens was coming back late that night to anchor offshore. They need have no fear of abandonment or isolation.

* * * *

It was after supper, and the two women were sitting in the glow of the fire.

"I'm so thankful, Sophie, that there are no wolves or bears on the island, the snakes are harmless, the Indians pacified, and one can safely go away for weeks leaving one's house unlocked. The one thing that does alarm me is the idea of fire — those stories of wooden houses being burned to the ground in less than three minutes. Are you quite sure you understand the furnace?"

"Of course. Anyway, we do sleep on the ground level upstairs, at the back anyway. But we will take care, darling mama, because this is such a heavenly place to live. I feel so happy here, and we couldn't descend to Noons again, could we?"

"Could any house burn in this terrific rain, do you think?" They stopped talking to listen to the slosh and hiss of the endless downpour, through which not even the sound of the sea could be heard. The grey, granite boulders of the fireplace looked ugly and cold even now, when they framed crackling, sparkling driftwood.

"Shall we paint it white, do you think?" Caroline mused.

They went on making plans, enjoyably, with long pauses, until it was time to go to bed, adjusting the oil cooker, as James had instructed them, and shutting down the furnace. Hot water bottles were filled, downstairs lights switched off. They lay in their own bedrooms. Caroline, after peering out through the rain, was sure she could just make out *Woodwind's* riding lights, and knew that someone was watching over them.

Chapter 7

THE NEXT NIGHT CAROLINE LAY AWAKE, listening this time to the gale. She heard the arpeggio of the wind swelling through the woods, the orchestration was superb, lingering chords were drawn from the sea as it pounded the roots of the house. For the third time there came the crash of a big tree falling. Supposing anything happened, she thought. What a long way off the neighbours are. Loggers and fisherman on the next point. Supposing I died, what would Sophie do? Would she live on here alone, like Mary? I believe she would. Growing mossier and mossier with the trees in the orchard, the wretched child. She seems to belong to it all much more than I do. Rooting, branching, blossoming.

The house shuddered again, under the wind and the waves. Just as well, Caroline, reflected, that Timothy had taken *Woodwind* around to Fulford Harbour that afternoon. Timothy and Sophie? She had sometimes thought — and Sophie ought to marry a man much older than herself of whom she was fond. But who was Timothy? He must, of course, be thoroughly investigated. That quality of Peter Panishness could be so infuriating in an older man. Looks he did have; family, at least, the Bryces'; some money, she supposed, though probably not much. But stability? Some aroma of the distillery, possibly gun-running? But they would have an interest in boats in common. She drifted back into an uneasy sleep, half-waking to an idea that later on she might sell Arbutus Point and they could all three go back to Europe.

Come daylight, what was a huge sea for these landlocked waters was running, and as soon as breakfast was finished, the Pomfrets hurried down to their beach. They climbed up on the rocks to stare at the monstrous waves. Grey waters were rolling and heaving around them, tree trunks and pieces of lumber rolled shorewards, tied with ribbons of kelp twenty feet long. The bladdered kelp ends bobbed in the trough of the waves like dark little heads. Snuff-coloured ducks, black and white ducks, grey divers with long graceful necks, all seemed to be enjoying themselves, and Sophie again wished that she knew their names. A garland of gulls flashed and wheeled overhead. Downwind, gulls screamed from precipices of clouds, while intent black cormorants skimmed the water.

" 'But resign this land, at the end, resign it, to its true owner, the tough one, the seagull,' " Caroline quoted with relish.

Her daughter looked at her and laughed. Then, seizing a large piece of bark which the sea had flung in at her feet, she shouted that she would never leave the beach empty handed. Always carry back bits of wood for the fire. Wet salvages, she prompted her mother, which must then be dried.

"Isn't the water cold? Edna says even in the summer it's as cold as ice."

"In the summer!" Caroline shrieked like one of the gulls. "In the summer. I thought this would be a kind of wild-west Lido. How I hate cold water."

"I suppose *Moppet* wouldn't be able to live in a sea like this. But as soon as it calms down I'll take her round the beaches to collect bark."

They pulled each other over piles of driftwood onto the strip of white beach. "I thought at first that this clamshell was coral," said Caroline. "We must dig for clams when there is a low tide. They live a foot down, Rose says, so it will be hard work."

"Those are the things that squirt through holes in the sand?"

"Yes, and seriously, we simply must begin to live off the country. I wish we had oysters here, there are so many at the north end. But they're so big they would probably be better cooked. Oyster stew, fried oysters?"

"Mother, Tim says your cheese paring is just a game."

"An eye to the main chance, perhaps? Anyway, my dear, it's unintelligent to be wasteful and not exploit your surroundings. I admire thrift, it's an art making the best of things."

"Are you feeling quite well, Mama?"

They stood awhile, watching the gulls blow about the sky. The tide was beginning to fall, leaving the beach littered with all kinds of wrack. Caroline picked up two giant floats, like beads, lost from some fisherman's net, and a nice bit of cork with a hole through the middle. These she strung on a length of seaweed to carry home, meaning to use them for something or other later. Then, from the kelp strewing the beach in glistening coils, she selected a short thong.

"What a lovely whip! It's time that you had a good beating."

She laid about her daughter whose screams, mingling with the bird's cries, were caught and scattered by the cold, rollicking wind.

Then it was Sunday, the days having vanished somehow. At the Pomfrets' there were desperate preparations for church, because all the right clothes had somehow been mislaid.

They hurried up the drive to their rendezvous with the female Noons at the mailbox, but paused beside the pond to regain a little breath. The mallard drake swam alone, his wife perhaps on a nest hidden among the brambles and rushes.

"Look!" Sophie pointed across the pond, where among a scattering of sunshine and shade, shaken down from the branches of the great fir, a doe was poised. She stood staring at them over her shoulder, showing the taut arch of her lovely neck. With a flick of white scut she took off over a windfall, and crashed away through a thicket of salal. Sophie sighed, feeling she said, from what she had just seen, that she had been to church already.

"Lovely, lovely! But darling, we must hurry. It will never do to keep Edna waiting. And let's hope the sermon won't dispel your illusions."

Caroline tugged her new grey cap a little more rakishly over one eye, and muttered the word "venison."

"I wonder," said Sophie, trotting after her mother, "if those white flowers could be trilliums? They're supposed to have three petals."

"Isn't that what the Noons used to call their cottage? Before Mallow so facetiously called it Trinity Cottage? Now it's called Holly House."

"And look at the moss on those enormous boulders. Have you ever seen anything so green and soft?"

"Well, yes." Her mother stared at Sophie.

"It's sad that your mind is so urbanized," Sophie retorted. "And why are you always cross on your way to church?"

Caroline chuckled, but saved her breath until they had got to their mailbox, where they scrabbled for any papers or letters which would have arrived the previous day. It was nice to have a minute to recover before the car, driven by Edna and with Rose in the back, came around the bend.

"For once we're not late!" Caroline was triumphant, as she greeted the sister-in-law.

"We're all late, dreadfully late," Edna moaned, "so I must step on it." Rose, meanwhile, started telling Sophie how much she was missed — and Caroline too, of course.

"How do you like it after nearly a week? What have you been doing?"

"It's lovely!" exclaimed Sophie.

"It's hard work," said Caroline. "All I do is wash and cook and drag up driftwood and dig clams."

"When the sea gets calmer, I'd love to come round in *Moppet* and see you," Sophie went on.

"Oh, please do. And perhaps, once the spring has really come, we could open up the old trail. It's far quicker than getting to each other by road. What lovely pink cheeks!"

"I expect I'm pink all over from rushing up the drive after mama in my Sunday best. Rose, we saw a deer by the pond."

"One of God's beautiful creations," Edna wafted back at them. As they flew over the bridge above Fulford Harbour, Rose pointed to the white flock of launches and fish boats below.

"Alan must be busy down there."

"Who's Alan?"

"He's a swell person, much more Canadian than most of the men here. He owns the boat yard, and works very hard at it. He was in the navy."

"Rose ought to have gone to live in the Prairies," Edna grumbled. "She likes everything Canadian."

"Well, I do sometimes think one might as well be living in Cheltenham as here."

They're all a bit crotchety, Sophie thought, and wondered why. She was relieved when they drew up outside the brown and white church, which stood in its neat garden of headstones, among budding live-oak trees. There was no one about, and the final bell was tolling, solemn and slow, each stroke seeming to hesitate for a second. They hurried up the path, to be met by one or the other of the Stanway twins as they entered the porch, beautiful and subdued in his Sunday best. He conducted them to a pew right up in front, winking at Sophie. Edna left them here, and slipped into her place among the choir. The bell stopped short, and Ambrose Mallow, at the organ, wound up an intricate improvisation.

"A minute more and it would have been the Kerry Dancers," Caroline whispered to Sophie, who was gazing at the moving tree shadows on the dull, green glass of the east window. It was nice, she was thinking, to be sitting here quietly, in the dim church, and to look up through that underwater colour. Though perhaps, when she was as old as Aunt Mary, she would present a stained glass window — the keel of St. Peter's fishing boat above a heavy net, full of silver and tinted fish, some rainbow-coloured ones slipping through the mesh, strings of bubbles rising through opalescent water to the surface, where forms could be half-seen leaning from the boat. Perhaps, even a few of those purple plush starfish on the sea floor, among a thicket of brown kelp.

Caroline crossly nudged her to rise for the first hymn, and she caught a smile from the vicar.

'And did those feet in ancient times,' sounded in the church. An ache went through her for that English green and pleasant land. But then at once she thought, This is a pleasant land, too, and it couldn't be greener.

After the usual kind of matins had been going on for awhile, the Vicar, serious and massive, stood by the chancel steps, talking to the children, in particular, about mental fights and chariots of fire while Sophie settled back to listen and learn.

Outside, at last, they met again all the people they had so recently met for the first time, and then got back into the car and were driven to the Noons' for lunch. James, his loins girt in a tablecloth, was basting the Sunday roast. Quickly, Rose gave another whisk to the batter, and thrust the Yorkshire pudding into the oven.

"Darn it," she was laughing, "there's no escaping the land of our birth today. You have cooked the beef beautifully, dear, and the potatoes are good and brown. I'm sure they couldn't do better in the green and pleasant homeland." She dispatched an apple pie into the oven to join the Yorkshire pudding. James began to fan himself with Sophie's hat.

"I'm simply worn to a shadow, it has been a busy morning," he quavered. "Let's have some beer. You see, Caroline, I'm not really domesticated like most of the men out here. I never batched, but seem always to have been married — in the best English sense. So I do find cooking most trying. But Edna, dear, I did manage to start the seed bed, after I brought in the sawdust and did the animal chores."

"Oh, isn't James marvellous, Mother?" Sophie was fervent. Then she added hungrily, "nothing gives one such an appetite as church."

"Only twenty minutes," promised Rose, passing round the beer. "What did you think of the sermon, Sophie? You were sitting very still."

"It was a wizard sermon."

"Till we have built Jerusalem?" mused Caroline, who was unravelling one of Aunt Mary's jerseys, preparatory to re-knitting it. "There are plenty of children of Israel in Britain already, the work must be about completed."

"My mother, the fascist," said Sophie. "Just wait till you hear her on our comrades in the USSR and the betrayed Baltic states. It's a marvel we weren't shut up in the Isle of Man during the war."

"No wonder Caroline and Timothy get on so well," said Edna, glancing up from a picture of emaciated European children in *LIFE*. "But I do wish Mr. Stanway wouldn't talk down to us as if we were children."

"Why is Mr. Stanway supposed to be fascist?" Sophie asked with interest. "I thought Uncle James said he was a communist?"

"All I said was that he takes a lot of interest in the atomic bomb," said James, rather mysteriously.

Chapter 8

"WHAT A RELIEF NOT to have to endure that incessant bloody telephone!" remarked Caroline one day, when she and Sophie were eating their leisurely breakfast in the nook. "I still hear those longs and shorts ringing with variations in my head. Here at least, at last we have a phone all to ourselves."

"Have some more toast, Mother. Uncle Jay certainly did a spiffy job cleaning up the stove."

Caroline nodded, so Sophie got up and laid down two slices of brown bread on the shining top of the cooker, being careful to keep any crumbs from getting into the cracks.

"Mind you don't let it flare again, Sophie."

"I didn't. It was you! It was you who went away and forgot it, you who let the porridge boil all over the stove, you who turned it too high in the first place to hurry the kettle, and then said afterwards, 'Now see what you made me do.' "

"Don't argue, child. You grow more like your great aunt every day. Go and make the beds, it gives me asthma. I'll wash up and listen to the news."

"The BBC direct from London," jeered Sophie, in an ultra English voice.

"Not at this time of day. It will be the CBC pausing for station identification." Directly Sophie had gone out of the room, Caroline untied the blue bows of the nook curtains, snatched them down, and bundled them into a cupboard.

She had felt at first they had been amusing, but now she could see no reason for curtains in a place where no one except the sun looked in. They could be used to make hostess aprons or some delicious little garment of the more intimate sort for the next rummage sale. She tackled the washing up, singing as she worked, and leaving the crockery to drain in the rack, though she did dry the silver.

I'm much better tempered, she found herself thinking, since we came to live here. I do wonder what Sophie does with the banana skins. She had been about to throw them in the cooker, but stopped herself just in time. One could dump them in the sea, perhaps, but then they would come back. Ah, the furnace must be the answer — it needed stoking in any case. Lovely that there was lots of dry cordwood down there.

Going down to the basement, she heard the clang of the furnace door. "Sophie," she called, "is that you?"

"No Mum," a falsetto voice answered, and James appeared, tonsure first.

"Oh good morning, James dear. Did you spend the night down there?"

"You have forgotten," he said accusingly, "that Stokes and I are going to do the drains today."

"A pox on my memory! Have you had breakfast?"

"Hours ago. I took Edna hers in bed. She was rather cross this morning. But if there's any coffee left. . . ."

"Hullo, 'ullo, Uncle James!" Sophie appeared, "Did you say coffee?"

They sat in the kitchen while a new brew got going, and James explained how he would begin on the grease trap while waiting for Stokes, who would probably want to open up the septic tank. "I shall need one of you to give me a hand."

"Okay, I'll help," offered Sophie.

"If it wasn't raining, I would make sandwiches and go off for a walk," Caroline shamelessly said. "That is, if there were anywhere to walk except up logging trails which only come to dead ends, in this land of eternal Christmas trees."

"She doesn't like smells," Sophie explained. "But you've still got a lot of unpacking to do, mama, that will keep you out of the way."

James started to tell Sophie what they must do. "I will need lots of hot water poured down the sink when I've ladled out the trap. Can you let me have some chloride of lime, I wonder?"

"There's a drum of it in the outside comfort station," put in Caroline. "What a perfect name for a privy."

James laughed happily. Caroline's curious remarks had, at first, rather shocked him. In the old days, he remembered, Rose, too, had had a tendency to the same sort of indiscreet flippancy, but Edna had managed to eradicate it, with her long, pale stare. Since the Pomfrets' arrival, a pleasant, relaxed vulgarity was once more beginning to tinge her remarks.

"Better not use it at all," Sophie warned, "in case the drains can't be fixed and the comfort station has to be kept decent. Oh, that must be Mr. Stokes."

"Thank goodness," said Caroline, failing to escape before a red-faced, squat man shouldered his way in and seized her by the hand.

He turned to James, who was, he announced, his side-kick. He too had a cup of coffee and then the men went into the vegetable garden, where the septic tanks were buried.

"Where are the nook curtains?" But her mother was scurrying through the sitting room on her way to the safety of upstairs.

In a moment, James could be seen again, standing on the porch and pulling on overalls, and adjusting an ARP gas mask. Then he removed the wooden lid of the grease trap under the kitchen window. He had a bucket and bailed out evil-smelling liquid, which had a crust on it all too reminiscent of the breakfast porridge. Sophie put on her overalls, and went out to help.

Turn by turn they carried the foul bucketsfull to the edge of the kitchen garden and tipped them out. From the far side, Stokes cheered them on. At last, all was empty, the greasy froth, the inky soup smelling of death. Only sad fronds of black slime hung down from the inlet pipe. These Sophie detached with an old broom. Then she went indoors and cascaded boiling water down the sink while Jim whited the sepulchre with an ample dredging of lime, and replaced the lid.

"It seems a shame to use it again," sighed Sophie, giving her hands a cursory wash in the sink. Stokes came in too, and they sat down to cigarettes and a couple of bottles of beer.

"The smell seems to be getting worse, doesn't it, Uncle Jim?"

"Ah, that's coming from Stokes' department now. We'll go off and get it sorted out."

Refusing her help, they returned to the kitchen garden, and she started to get lunch ready.

Caroline, meanwhile, in a paroxysm of hay fever, was removing a final layer of Aunt Mary's garments from the wardrobe. The smell of mothballs was detestable. How ever did one get rid of it? She arranged the purple silk negligee in a box, intending to send it to Edna, and then she looked around, wondering if she could find a suitable present for Rose. Remembering the bare, white austerity of her bedroom, she decided it must be intentional. But nevertheless, she might enjoy one of the little old Persian rugs on her wooden floor. For James, she had planned a bracket clock which she did not much like. All these presents could be wrapped in the nook curtains.

"Mary wouldn't object," she said to herself, "and if there's trouble over the inventory later, I can always borrow them back." She returned heroically to the wardrobe, and cast out a pile of hats. These, and other shapeless apparel could be sent to Moya, who might be able to sell them, along with a sealskin coat, which lacked charm. All the other garments she and Sophie might be able to alter and use. Except for the really improbable things, bundles and bundles left over for Britain, woolen combinations, pink corsets, scarves. She tried in vain to smother a fresh paroxysm of sneezing, with the paper hankies she now used to save laundry. Perhaps she hadn't yet acquired the knack, too often she blew right through them. And when she dropped them about the house and garden, they looked so devastatingly squalid. They made her think of all those places in Vancouver and Victoria where they festooned bushes, caught up in webs, slowly disintegrating. The charms of a crisp square of Irish linen, neatly embroidered, or a flutter of lace-edged lawn, could hardly be exaggerated. A snowy crumple, impregnated with Chanel, which, if cast in one's wake, could be retrieved without shame and restored with grace. The idea of these tissues being picked up made her laugh and shudder. She folded the last pair of drawers in the last cardboard box, and decided it was time for lunch. She opened the door and was immediately assailed by a fearful smell, wafting up the staircase.

"Shades of Aunt Mary come to haunt us?"

"My poor, poor Caroline!" retorted an unexpected voice from the open front door. "It is I, Timothy, who comes to haunt you. But can you really smell anything, with your poor small nose so red and runny? None but I would haunt you when you look like that."

She blinked at him with streaming eyes. "You can smell something awful, can't you, Timothy. What is it?"

"Yes, can't I!" he agreed with feeling. "But then I wonder if it isn't part of my charm, my very special aura."

"This can't be just the drains."

"Nothing to worry about — only Noon and your lovely daughter, stirring up the grease trap. Of Stokes I did not enquire. I expect he has unearthed traces of Aunt Mary's past. This is no place for you, Caroline, so I shall carry you off for an al fresco lunch on board. Omelette aux fines herbes, bananas and cream, coffee. Rose stood me some thick cream and sped me on my way, bless her virgin heart."

She breathed gratefully. "Alright. After all, we needn't be long. My hay fever is devastating. Just wait while I put my face on — such as it is."

So they stole away to slip out in the dinghy to *Woodwind*, lying at anchor in the sweet-smelling bay.

"A trickle of brandy because of the hay fever?" he suggested when they had finished lunch.

"Thank you, Tim. Will it help the feeling of guilt, too?"

"I wouldn't know, not being burdened with a sense of sin."

"Oh well, Sophie is so wonderfully competent, don't you agree? Also intelligent, and even, at times, quite beautiful."

He laughed lightly, "My dear, there is no need to sing your daughter's praises so fervently. She is, of course, incomparable."

Caroline looked a trifle startled and then laughed too. "Please, a cigarette." she murmured. "And I was only thinking aloud, not singing."

Despite her profession of guilt, they sat talking for quite a while, coming to the conclusion that they must have stayed at the same village in the Tyrol at the same time in '37. More recently, he had been in Mexico, able to indulge, once more, his passion for travel. It was peaceful and intimate, talking to one of similar experience and disposition, and it was with regret that Caroline at last said she must return. Together they tidied away the remains of the meal, and she asked casually, "Haven't you got an interest in a distillery somewhere?"

"Oh, that's just a joke. It means people think I might be running a still on one of the islands. Of course I do cash in on a lot of people's liquor permits, which lets me give a few parties. And oblige, with great profit to myself, the summer visitors. I wish you would apply for a liquor book, Caroline. You might just as well be co-operative."

"Certainly I shan't be able to afford a cellar, so you may as well have my permit. Show me what I have to do."

"Sure," said Timothy with a grin. "It's very simple. One writes a note for the bearer, that's all, and hands over the book, and one is rewarded in kind at some later time."

* * * *

"Oh rats! We saw you deserting the stinking ship," Sophie called out as they crept guiltily into the back of the house, which was now redolent of chloride of lime.

"This is what prison smells like, Mr. Spens," said Caroline darkly. She then looked at her disheveled daughter suspiciously. "Are you sure you are quite clean, darling? You must have been through quite a lot."

"Well, I have washed. But it will be half-an-hour before the water gets warm enough for another bath. Uncle Jim has had his."

Stokes wafted in at this point, also obviously in need of a bath. "Not all the perfumes of Arabia can sweeten that little hand," Timothy stared at Stokes' large, red paw, now thrust out to take a doughnut from the ready-laid tea table. He and Jim were wearing the superior and affable expressions of men whose day has been well spent. Ignoring Spens, James turned his avuncular attention to Sophie.

Chapter 9

"I HAVE SEEN THE LADY APRIL bringing in the daffodils," Caroline announced, as Sophie, hair a-shine, came in from the garden with an armful of saffron and green. "Lots of leaves, I hope, they need lots of leaves."

"Sure, there's lots of leaves, why wouldn't there be? I believe its stopped raining for good, Mom, let's go for a small picnic in *Moppet.* It's quite safe if you sit still."

"Sorry darling, but I'm going to doze on the porch in the rocking chair, and warm my old bones in a patch of sun until the cow arrives."

Sophie thought for a moment that her mother must be referring to a female caller, the doctor's wife perhaps, but then it dawned on her. "The cow! Hell, I'd forgotten! I'll stop and help, of course."

But Caroline insisted that this was not necessary. The cow was middle-aged, quiet and respectable, with lovely teats. And Stokes, her late owner, was bringing her in the truck. James would be there to help, of course. "You go for your picnic, but be careful to keep inshore, and if it gets rough, beach *Moppet* and walk back."

Sophie dropped one of her infrequent kisses on top of her mother's head and went off to make herself peanut butter sandwiches. Such a quiet day, she thought, as she then hauled the little boat down into the water. Timothy had long ago kept his word, and caulked and painted it.

Her 'moppet'. She admired it before she stowed away her lunch, the fishing tackle, a rag for polishing the spoon, and a foot of iron bar with which to kill any unfortunate fish. She was wearing her semi-new and wonderful Cowichan sweater, with its scattered, all-over pattern of brown birds and beasts, which Moya had procured with some of the money realized form the sale of Aunt Mary's clothes.

The sea was sparkling and calm, no boats or people. The only sound was the lap of water. She sighed with happiness, thinking how much she loved these islands, all of which she could now name, even the American ones — San Juan, Orcas, Waldron, Stewart, and the rest. Their volcanic peaks were submerged in the blue sea up to their necks. Staring at them now, she remembered the rector's term, 'A delicious archipelago.'

Skimming along in her cockleshell, she gazed at the limpid green water along the rocky shore, where the coves, white-floored with clamshell, extended under the sea. A squawk make her look up. A bald eagle rocked above her on its wide-spanned wings. She could clearly see its white feathered head, not bald at all, and the light underlining of its wings. Thunderbird, the totem eagle, hunting fish!

Further out from the shore the sea, streaked with royal blue, flicked baubles of sunlight at her. Every mountain was shaggy with timber. The twisting arbutus trees, lower down, lent a kind of enchantment to the shoreline; suggestive, even to Sophie, of half-remembered classical nymphs.

But her attention was turning to more concrete matters. She shipped the oars and reached for her fishing line, wound round a piece of wood. Unhooking the spoon, she polished it diligently, and dropped it and the sinker over the stern, with some forty feet of line following. Then she placed the reel between her feet and started to row again. She was well out of sight of home and making for the small island where she planned to eat her picnic. But she could still just see the Noon's clearing when suddenly her reel leapt, and scarcely remembering to ship the oars, she began to wind in. It felt like quite a large fish, but gave little fight — a few tugs and she had dragged it aboard. Big eyes in a large head, a spiny back which was pretty and pink-green, horrible to have to bludgeon this attractive creature, but she supposed that having started on such a pursuit she must now complete it. Two blows with the crowbar, and she made herself extract the hook. If the fish was not, after all, edible, how pointlessly would it have lost its life! It shuddered as she pushed it into the stern with her foot, and she decided she had had enough for one day, and would simply row on to the island. Over her shoulder she made out a small and sheltered beach, where she could land. She hauled her boat high and dry, being uncertain about the state of the tide, these waters came and went regardless of the laws of nature. She really must remember to ask Timothy to explain the system, as well as another mystery which her mother puzzled over — why there were tides in the Adriatic but not in the Mediterranean. He would know, being so much cleverer than anyone realized.

She flopped down on a dry log, tired from so much rowing and unhappy to find that she had brought too little food. The butterless sandwiches were already dry. How fortunate the cow had already arrived. For Caroline had been unlucky with her shopping this week. Driving to Ganges with the Noons, she had placed the usual order, to be delivered next day by truck, but almost nothing had been available. Lots of prunes and tea, no fats, no cheese, no meat. Most people were giving their meat coupons to the Red Cross to allow more meat to go overseas. Anyway, little seemed to have reached the island. Finishing what she had, Sophie rolled onto the beach, lit a cigarette, and stared up at the blue sky. A woodpecker was working industriously on some hollow tree close by, the solitary clacking making her think suddenly how much she missed the birdsongs of England. But then she loved the timelessness of this place. It must have looked just the same when the Haidas swooped down in war canoes, she had been told, to kill and enslave the local Indians. And when captains Cook and Vancouver sailed here. An enchanted country, full of ghosts and a long history she was beginning to understand had so very little to do with her own people.

A slight noise made her quickly alert. A tall young man with flaming ginger hair was staring at her with an expression of surprise. He was freckled, and clad in a striped blue and white singlet, and flannel trousers rolled up to the knees. He looked older than her, but less than thirty.

"Say, I didn't mean to startle you," he apologized, "but you scared me for a moment. Thought I must have happened on a mermaid."

"Am I trespassing? Terribly sorry."

"You're not trespassing. I don't own the foreshore rights. Could you be Miss Pomfret, from Arbutus Point?"

Sophie nodded, "Yes, Sophie."

"I'm Alan Graham. I've got a place just round the point. I'm living ashore these days."

"Oh, you live here? I was just going to explore the island. I thought it was empty. You must be the one who built *Woodwind*."

"Dad and I built her before the war," he answered, sitting down on a log beside her. "He died two years ago, so I came out of the Service as someone had to run the yard. We built minesweepers and lifeboats. But I'd been in the sick-bay with pneumonia, so I guess they weren't too sorry to get rid of me."

"After those days in the open boat, when your boat was sunk?"

"How ever did you hear that? Brother Spens, I guess. Do you like *Woodwind*?"

"Oh, she's beautiful."

"Will you come and meet my mother, and have tea?"

She accepted with pleasure, and they went first to make sure of *Moppet*'s safety.

"That's a small craft to go cruising in. A canoe would be safer in these waters. Oh! You caught a rock cod. Great to eat if you fillet it first."

"I've never filleted a fish, though I can clean one. Could you show me how?"

"We'll take it with us and do it at home." He hooked a finger through a gill, and then laughed. "I reckon you and your mother are having a tough time learning how to do things from us old timers."

"People are being most awfully kind," she protested. "I don't know what we should have done without the Noons' and Tim."

Following him along the narrow track through the salal, she told him how James was going to teach them to milk the cow. They went side by side through a wider clearing, where the underbrush had been cleared, where among moss and fallen leaves Easter lilies — erythronium, he called them — were growing delicately. Through a gap could be seen a bleached and silvery wood cottage which stood in a further clearing, backed by orange, twisted arbutus and the pale blue enamel of the sea. The window frames were painted grey, and a gull perched on the grey shingled roof. A few daffodils blew in a sunny wall angle.

Mrs. Graham was busy spreading kelp on borders. Wet, rubbery tubes slithered from the wheelbarrow beside her, and the smell of seaweed as they approached was strong. To wake her from this engrossing occupation, Alan called out, "Hey Mom, we've got a visitor."

She turned, and without surprise, came to meet Sophie, who had a few seconds to perceive how thin she was, and how the plaits of her hair braided round her head, once red, were now like lamb's wool. She was also wearing a Cowichan sweater, far older and more worn than Sophie's. They shook hands and moved on into the house.

"I'm also a visitor," she said. "In fact, I go back to my apartment in West Vancouver tomorrow. So I'm very glad you came today. At least I can give you a cup of tea. Alan, when batching, tends to produce a bottle of rum."

Sophie exclaimed with delight at the cottage — white kalsomined walls, unstained furniture, also white with scrubbing, a red and blue hooked rug ("my mother's"), and an enclosed stove where driftwood burned, and a comfortable black cat sleeping in front of it. Framed charts hung above shelves of books. By the blue-curtained window stood a gramophone. "What a perfect place! I do wish it was mine."

"Come and see the kitchen," Alan responded, and led her through to a second room, where he lit a rock-gas stove and put on a kettle. While they waited for it to boil he told her that there was water laid on, with a gas pump in the shed outside to pump it for the occasional shower, though he did have to be careful not to use to much in summer, and all sorts of other conveniences to please a modern mind.

Mrs. Graham joined them to make tea. "How lucky I made tea biscuits," she announced with satisfaction, and carried in a plate of them to the other room. Sophie, seeing what she had always known as scones, also expressed her delight. Then, looking hungrily at the stacked-up tray with a jar of honey included, she asked Alan if he lived on the island all alone, and if so, was he not sometimes rather cut off? Could he always get food?

"Yes, he's crazy enough to insist on it," his mother answered for him. "There's a good house at the Yard where his father and I used to live. But Alan put the foreman and his wife in it before he went off to the war, and now he's allowing any friends who want to use it for parties and things."

"Too many people at the Yard," muttered Alan. "All day long asking questions. Always wanting some darned thing or other. People off the boats, you know, they seem to think I'm secretary of the Yacht Club. And this place is only thirty mintues from the Yard by launch. I can get most of my meals there, and peace and quiet here. When Spens is around he lives on his boat there, and he's quite happy to talk to possible clients and give them drinks."

"How is Timothy?" Sophie asked. "We haven't seen him for some time."

"Oh, he always was a restless sort of guy. He goes off for weeks on *Woodwind*, probably collecting on liquor permits or something of the sort. He gets them from every female in the province."

"You know how strongly I disapprove," said his mother .

"What can I do?" protested Alan. "After all, I'm only obliging a friend. I don't get a rake-off, except sometimes the odd bottle."

"Good gracious! Is that what he does? I certainly hope you don't aid and abet him at the Yard. Suppose he's caught?"

"Most people think the liquor law is dumb. And if he is caught he won't mind making a martyr of himself just to show how dumb it is. But didn't you know?"

"No, or at least I thought it was a joke when everyone talked about his still."

"Sure, that really is a joke, or at least I hope so."

"Poor Tim, he enjoys being a mystery man," put in Mrs. Graham.

Sophie turned to her. "I suppose he and I have always talked about boats. There's so much I want to know."

"How about letting me show you round the Yard one day soon? I'd certainly enjoy it."

"I thought you said you had too many people there, all asking questions about boats," Sophie responded.

"But it isn't about boats that they ask questions. If they did I could answer them better. Do come."

"I'd very much like to, thank you. But gracious me, it's nearly five o'clock, if I don't get home my mother will believe I'm swept away in *Moppet*. I've had such a heavenly time, being here and meeting you both, I really did enjoy it."

"Wait one minute — I'll fillet that rock cod and you can watch, and then you'll know how to do it next time."

Deftly, he sliced up the fish in the little kitchen, and then put it into a paper bag. Before she could thank him, he disappeared, muttering something, and was back again with a book. "This is something you might like to borrow — *Captain Cook's Voyages*. I think you'd like it as much as I do."

She thanked him again, and begged Mrs. Graham to call at Arbutus Point next time she came over from Vancouver. Then they all went down to the wharf to look at the launch, wide-beamed and seaworthy. Alan suggested that he would run her back home in it, towing *Moppet*, but she insisted that she would row home and watch the sunset. So Alan walked her back through the wood, after a fond farewell from Mrs. Graham, past the lily glade again, recounting how, in his childhood, the first picnics of the year had been lily picnics. They had gone to remote islands, where no sheep grazed, and gathered lilies in armfuls.

"But I really think these are my favourites." He picked and gave her a small flower she had not previously noticed, purple and hooded, which smelt delicious. "It's a ladyslipper."

Together, they lifted *Moppet* down to the water, said goodbye to each other as if they had been friends for years, and waved again as she pulled out, and he called after her, "Let's have a cruise around the islands one day."

"Lovely, Alan. Soon."

He stood watching, as she rowed over a campion-pink sea and disappeared around the point.

By the time she got home, it was cold and almost dark. She stowed the boat away and went up to find an empty house. The barn perhaps? In the adjacent cow stall a storm lantern showed James giving Caroline her first milking lesson. Sophie was amused to see her mother dressed for the part, in baggy overalls and a beret. She was crouched by the side of a brownish-cream cow, a Jersey, to whom James made encouraging noises.

"No," he said patiently, as the cow shed a spattering of milkdrops into the pail. "Press down with your fingers in turn, as if you were playing the flute."

"I am doing that, you fool. This is just how I play the flute. She must have gone dry, there's no milk inside her."

"Look, I'll show you again."

As they changed places, Caroline caught sight of her daughter.

"Sophie, hullo! At last! How like you to go off for the entire day, leaving me all alone to cope with this monstrous animal. You're fearfully late."

To her mother's cross words, Sophie answered amiably, "Mother, you are the limit. You know you told me to go as Uncle James was coming to help."

She patted his bald head affectionately, and then turned to the cow, and did the same. "Isn't she sweet? I caught a fish, Mum, and then I had tea with some people on the little island."

"Really?" Caroline murmured, without much interest, and bending down to what results James was getting.

"Let me have another tweak, James. You give her some more mash to keep her quiet." She was determined to extract those four magic white jets from the unresponsive teats. But the cow shifted her weight just as they changed places, and flicked Caroline across the face with her tail, as if defying her.

"No more canned milk," Sophie said happily. "Whatcha' know?"

"Do keep quiet, you're taking her mind off, no wonder she's so difficult. Go and cook supper if you want something to do. James is staying, so you'd better open a can or two."

"Okay, and we'll eat my fish, as well." She went off to prepare a banquet of rock cod eked out by a couple of cans of chowder.

Chapter 10

THE NOONS AND POMFRETS were going to dine with the Mallows, and then go on to a fancy dress dance, being held at the church hall in aid of the Red Cross. The Mallows, who had run the local little theatre before the war, still had quantities of costumes, and it was arranged that they would all dress up after dinner, if they felt like it.

James had come to call for the Pomfrets before this event, and he and Sophie were watching the final stripping of Cow. He commended his pupil, adding rather sadly, "You are so proficient, Caroline, that I don't think you will need my help any more. There's a great deal that wants attending to at home — including Edna. But perhaps I can still come round sometimes and give you a hand with the garden. How's it doing?"

"We've got peas, lettuce, and carrots and spinach already," answered Sophie. "What we do is dig a bit and seed it as we go. Mother is saving the potato eyes to plant, in her frugal manner. We've quite adopted the BC view that a garden means only a vegetable garden, as you see."

They all three abandoned the cow and went into the house, where Sophie proudly showed James the firm, yellow pound of butter which she had made that morning, using a small glass churn and endless patience. To make it had taken the same time as the Pastoral Symphony on the radio, which James considered too long, though he agreed that the results looked quite dandy.

"Caroline," he said with difficulty, "we are wondering if you would sell us the spare skim milk, now that Mavis is beginning to dry up?"

"Well, I have been thinking about buying a brace of pigs, but perhaps I should wait a little. Yes, of course, come and collect it once or twice a week. And that will give you an excuse for coming to see us. In exchange, maybe you would do the odd hour's digging, and then we can plant our potatoes."

He agreed cheerfully, and bustled them into getting ready to leave for the Mallows. Sophie touched up her mouth a deeper coral in front of the hall mirror. Caroline came and stood beside her.

"Sheep. Now, do you think the fences are good enough, James?" She thought that Sophie, in her brown crêpe dress, made over from one of Aunt Mary's, looked slim — nearly as slim as herself, in black.

"I'll have a word with the Sheepbreeder's Association, and get someone to go round and look," answered James, staring with admiration at the women then accompanying them, one on each arm, to the car.

They drove in to pick up the lady Noons, and found Rose already in her coat under the porch, and looking rather worried. Greeting them affectionately, she said that Edna was just coming. "She's put on her fancy dress, Jim."

"Oh hell! Why couldn't she wait like the rest of us? Get in, Rose, we're going to be late."

The front door flew open and Edna appeared. She was carrying her musquash over one arm, and on the other a long-handled, idiotic flower basket, containing bundles of dried lavender. She blew kisses to all of them. Her ample bosom, Caroline could see, was shrouded in a fichu, the rest of her person panniered in Aunt Mary's purple tea gown, and a beribboned mop cap to top this off. A delicate wisp of an apron, in which Caroline recognized her nook curtains, completed the resemblance to Yardley's Lady of the Lavender Water.

"Oh well done! How nice you look," she cried, while Rose clapped vigorously, though James remained silent. She really did look sweet, quite softened and roguish. "Yes, yes, most pretty, my dear," James at last allowed. "But do put on your coat, we're late."

Caroline being already in her usual seat, Edna had to squeeze into the back, emitting a cloud of lavender water mixed with moth balls. They all coughed a little, and felt relieved when they got to the Mallows, and James sounded the horn to warn their hosts. From above answered the already alcoholic whoops of Ambrose, who was descending the steps with a dog to meet them. Up in the hall Moya said, "I've got the costumes in my room, people, do you want to come and see them before we eat? But, Edna, you are changed already. How lovely!"

Mallow kissed her hand extravagantly, "Mrs. Yardley, I presume?"

"No Ambrose, Lavender Lady."

"You must always wear that colour, dear Lavender Lady," and he winked at his wife as Edna was replying, "But I nearly always do."

"Oh, oh, ah-tishoo!" sneezed Caroline, for whom the closed car had been too much. She searched fruitlessly in her bag for another hankie.

"Ambrose, get Caroline a drink right away, and it may stop. And a box of tissues. Look Sophie, I want you to try this on."

Moya lifted a spangled fairy dress off the bed. It was a pale electric blue, with a pair of silver wings attached.

"Gawd!" snuffled Caroline, unable to say more, and appalled to see Sophie reaching for it with every appearance of delight. She was taking off her brown dress when Ambrose came back with a tray of glasses. He thrust it at his wife, uttering falsetto screams of outraged modesty, and hastened to join James trying on his garments in another room.

Caroline sniffed and sipped, sniffed and sipped, until her sneezes diminished. She picked up from the pile of garments on the bed a peasant dress with a raggedly cut hem, faded brown and yellow, and with a laced bodice which made her think of Cinderella. "It's too short," she muttered, "but let's see, there was an old woman as I heard tell, who went to market her eggs for to sell — went to sleep on the king's highway — up came a pedlar — cut her petticoats up to her knees, poor old woman she began to sneeze. So all I'll need is some eggs in a basket."

Moya, listening fascinated to this soliloquy, offered some china ones. Rose meanwhile unearthed a pair of black silk pajamas, and, discarding her marocain, pulled them on.

" 'So free, so free and easy on the drawers,' " she misquoted from the cigarette advertisement, and looking so happy that Moya could not bear to tell her that they were her own nightwear.

Instead, she gave her a black scarf to tie around her head, completing, with a wreath of artificial flowers round her neck, the transformation.

"We could be Night and Day," Edna remarked benignly. "But what are you going to wear, Moya?"

"I'll keep Rose company in another pair of pajamas. But do look at this child! Isn't she perfect?"

Sophie pirouetted in a pair of worn silver ballet shoes which just happened to fit, and beamed at them radiantly.

All decked out, they now trooped through the hall into the big room, where the radio played, and James, who had undergone a sea change, marched up and down. A fine set of whiskers, weepers in fact, adorned his chubby face, and he wore black cotton gloves, and a winged collar, encircled by a black cravat, and ancient morning coat, and a pair of black rubbers over his shoes. Tolling a dinner bell he now chanted, "Bring out your dead. The cash and carry funeral homes will help you out."

Moya and Rose, in their decent black, might be part-time mourners, or better still, mutes, he gleefully said — at union rates, of course.

Unheard in the general noise and laughter, Alan Graham came in and flashed a smile at Sophie before striding over to Moya. He looked as if he was meant to be a pirate, silk scarf round his head, pink shade over one eye. Through the uproar, he was introduced to Caroline, and at once returned to Sophie, pushing up his shade so that he could see her better.

"How cute your wings are. Perhaps I do, at last, believe in fairies."

Mallow handed round more drinks, and warmly agreed with his last remark. "It's really I who need the eyeshade, I saw the metamorphosis, it was a real event.'

In the little pause that followed, the radio made a portentous reference to Mos-cow, and "Yippee!" said someone, "What a swell name for your new cow, Caroline."

"A cow by any other name would smell sweeter, I'm afraid. But it's good. Mossy for short, perhaps."

"Moss rose might be nicer," suggested Edna, who was graciously sipping sherry.

"After me?" asked Rose.

"No, Rose dear, and don't drink any more cocktail."

"Oh sweet Lavender, let a girl have her fling."

"Ambrose," said Graham, looking guilty, "Tim wanted a word with you in the hall — I sort of forgot."

Then Mrs. Dobbs, the help for the evening, came in to say that supper was ready. Moya rounded up Edna, who was showing a tendency to loiter, as she heard the clinking of bottles from the far side of the door. They moved off into the kitchen, and were starting on tomato juice by the time

Tim and Mallow joined them. Tim wore his teddy bear overcoat and slithered over the floor because his bare feet were thrust in huge fur gloves.

"Winnie-the-Pooh," he announced, ruffling his normally smooth, fair hair, "Winnie-the-Pooh, the exoteric sailor, home from the deep to take part in the gaila."

"Gala," corrected Edna.

"If exoteric means tight, you're certainly right," burbled the undertaker. "Won't you be too hot if you spend the evening in that?"

"Well, perhaps I will," Tim agreed, kicking off his gloves.

"Oh," gasped Caroline, "did you touch me, Timothy? Under the table I mean. I've got a phobia about bare male feet. If you move them an inch, I shall scream. Do you know the strange young man with the vermilion hair and pink eyeshade, sitting next to Sophie?" she added in a whisper. "I didn't catch his name just now."

"Our strawberry blonde? Yes, m'dear, that is Andrew Ramsbottom," he lied. "Didn't you know he and Sophie were buddies? They walk out on the nearest desert island, and he gives her presents of fish. Just now I thought I heard him calling her his maple sugar."

"You brute, your foot touched me again."

"Not mine, no," he stared at her innocently. "Must be Bracken, I'm using him as a foot warmer. I do wonder why Ambrose hasn't dressed up. Why haven't you Ambrose?"

"Too infuriating, Tim, but I have literally nothing to wear."

"Nothing, my dear chap? And to think that there is a shop upon these premises, full to bursting with feather boas and tippets. How ambrosical. As is this delicious fruit salad, Moya."

Sophie now started to take some interest in the general conversation.

"Where have you been so long, Tim? We have missed you."

"A most unsuitable question for an old remittance man."

"And another person I haven't seen about," she turned to Moya, "is Fern. Is she off hunting?"

"She's in such an interesting condition that I've had to shut her up, poor dear. I'm thinking of changing her name to Fertility, and Bracken's to Fidelity. If I give you a puppy, what will you call it?"

"How about Simplicity? Then it could be Simple."

Half an hour later, Sophie and Alan left for the dance, with the others promising to follow soon. Walking down to the hall, they passed a line of cars, from a number of which came a merry noise of glass clinking against bottle, and siren voices offering drinks, all of which Alan sternly refused. Disappearing into a congested, little cloakroom Sophie combed her hair, and shaking out her wings went to find Alan, who was talking to the Vicar and the twins. These were clad in chef's aprons and holding sharp knives; she still could not tell them apart. Mr. Stanway asked her for the next waltz, and she promised dances to the twins, and then Alan claimed her. It was with a sigh of relief that she found they danced easily together.

About half the dancers were wearing fancy dress — or looking as if they might be. Lady Bryce had on a mandarin's coat, but as her face was always parchment yellow, and her hair tightly drawn back, it was impossible to tell which category she came under. Mrs. Stanway was wearing a Spanish shawl over black. Then there were enough drum majorettes for a parade, and Canadian Mounties, young men and women in sateen jackets and cowboy outfits, some of whom Sophie already recognized and who greeted her warmly.

The three-piece band was good and loud. Alan told her that they were brothers from a local family, descended from slaves escaped long ago from south of the border.

The next dance was a waltz and a twin could be heard declaring loudly that his old man sure had pull up there, as his father and Sophie moved onto the dance floor.

"I'm so glad you came as yourself," Sophie told him as they circled smoothly.

"I'm glad you came as yourself. We need more magic on the island. Too much of our glamour is derived from Hollywood. Goodness gracious! Look, here comes the rest of your party!"

A merry rabble was surging through the door.

"Shall we watch from the verandah?" suggested the rector. "Alan's there, and it's cooler."

In the glassed-in, and dimly lit porch they found Alan smoking his pipe and gazing intently at Caroline, who was carefully depositing her basket of China eggs in a corner before knotting the spotted red handkerchief under her chin and lunging away with Mallow, now sporting a topi from which streamed a cloud of green tulle. As a further concession, he wore sunglasses. Tim and Rose followed them onto the floor, Tim's pajamas anchored down by a massive pair of old fashioned, grey corsets. The suspenders twirled wildly about as he danced, neatly shod in off-white tennis shoes. Demure still in her decent black, Rose was clearly having a good time, beaming out of her wreath, and now and again tweaking Tim's suspenders to make him groan.

Behind her Sophie could see James, with Lady Lavender on his arm, sporting a battered top hat, and Moya, with her fiddle, going to join the parade which was beginning to form for the purpose of being judged.

Alan gave a shout of laughter at the sight. "Come on Sophie," and he dragged her off into an impromptu conga, also closely observed by Mrs. Stanway, Sir Ernest and Lady Bryce, and their group, who were in a huddle, trying to decide who was the winner of the fancy dress. Sophie was seized by one of the twins, and then, a minute later, by the other, who started to teach her some jitterbug steps. Before she could do more than watch, Tim cut in, and wafted her across the hall, trying out a number of steps, and then congratulating her on her performance — almost as good as her mother's.

Alan moved up to take her over once more, just as Sir Ernest demanded silence in order to announce the prize winners. After protracted and careful thought on the part of the committee, it had been decided that of all the beautiful and indeed amusing costumes presented for inspection, Mrs. James Noon's had been thought the most striking. Therefore, with great pleasure, he wished to announce that Mrs. Noon, as Lavender Lady, was winner of first prize. Would she please come forward and receive the — ah, indeed he might say — the fruits of her endeavour. There was a moment's silence, and then a great deal of polite clapping. Eagerly Edna tripped forward to receive from Mrs. Stanway the fruits, a box which proved to contain an attractive tea set of Californian pottery. She looked overcome with joy, and had to be removed, along with the carton, to the family car.

A fat lady of the fair got candies — a yard of them — and the third winner was the rector himself, rewarded by tobacco.

"Come on chaps, let's get organized!" said Mallow after all this was over. "We're going down to Tim's nightclub, and you won't need to bring any bottles. We'll have to take the cars."

"Shush!" said Tim. "Don't tell all the world."

Edna, already in her car, clutched her pottery and uttered little shrieks of excitement as they drove down to Fulford Harbour. There, in the old club, somebody seemed already to be having a party. Dancing figures passed across the lighted windows to the boogie-woogie of a juke box. A voice called out, as they trooped in. "For Pete's sake, Tim, get the barrel rolling, there's not a drop here."

Tim looked obliging, and quickly mingling his friends with the group of Norwegian Americans, who had come off their boat tied up at the wharf, took James and Mallow off to get bottles from *Woodwind.* James was still holding Edna's arm and her prize parcel, so she went with them, announcing that she would like to lie down on board for a little. So the three men went back to the club without her, clutching as many bottles as they could. Behind an improvised bar, Tim started to mix drinks deftly. "A dillar, a dollar, two bits for a swaller," Ambrose chanted, watching Tim pocket the American bills. A trickle of other fugitives from the dance kept coming into the club. Someone started up the jukebox.

"The next round is on the house," said Tim. It was at this moment that the light flickered and went out. In the silence they could hear a siren.

"It's okay, fellows," Alan said quietly through the darkness, "this is just one of Spen's private parties. No payments, remember."

The lights came on again, and the police sergeant, followed by his young constable, pushed through the crowd at the door. Caroline, looking round for Tim, was surprised not to see him.

"Hullo!" Mallow greeted the police irately, "Is it you having fun with the lights?"

"Now what's going on here? I seem to have broken up a nice little party. Are you Mr. Spens?" He was looking at Alan, who answered, "No, I'm Alan Graham. You must be the new sergeant. Mr. Spens is entertaining friends on my property, mostly visitors from the United States."

"You mean he's selling them liquor." He glanced round at the expectant crowd. "Don't any of you move." His eyes slid on. "Where is Mr. Spens? Go and check his boat, Constable."

"Where is he?" Sophie whispered to her mother.

"There goes *Woodwind* — what a silly fool."

Sophie was pale with excitement, listening to the distant motor.

"You had drinks here?" the sergeant was asking the Americans.

"Yes, sir, we certainly did." They glanced at the table.

"Cost you more, I reckon, than across the border?"

Looks of pained surprise appeared on their faces. "What are you getting at, Mister? We're invited here by Mr. Spens. It's a party, see?"

The younger policeman, trying not to grin, came back. "Sir, the boat *Woodwind* has put to sea. Looks like he's made his getaway clean, see."

The sergeant glared at him. "See? Sure, I see. A guy don't make a getaway unless he's gotta get away."

James began, "What did you say? My God, Edna, Edna!"

Rose kicked his ankle and Caroline began to laugh. "The explanation becomes quite simple," she cooed at the sergeant. "Mrs. Noon and Mr. Spens have gone off together for a moonlight sail."

"It's a funny way to carry on. But I'll see him in the morning — if he comes back." Saying no to a drink the sergeant huffed his way out followed by the friendly constable. But the party continued sporadically until all the bottles were empty. Then, as several boats had tied up to a float — the Bryces' *San Juan* among them — Alan led the remnants of the Mallows' party down there, all except James and Rose, who wanted to drive home quickly just in case Edna was returned. Alan assured Caroline that he would take her and Sophie home later. "I told Rose I would," he smiled at Caroline.

"It's very good of you, Mr. Ramsbottom."

Sophie looked with concern at her mother, wondering if she had not drunk too much gin. "This is Alan Graham, Mother, whom I told you about," she said very distinctly. They climbed down in Bryces' crowded cabin.

"Graham?" said Caroline. "Oh, really? Then I was misled. I'm glad to meet you under your proper name. Tim said you were Mr. Ramsbottom. I had to ask him because there was so much noise when we met that I could hardly hear, and he called you the local strawberry blonde. I wish Tim wouldn't get so juvenile in his cups."

"Well, anyway, and whoever I am, I'd love to take you home if I may."

"Ramsbottom indeed!" Sophie said merrily. "And Tim really is a yellow bellied sapsucker deserting us like that."

"What a delightful name for my nephew," beamed Lady Bryce, who joined them just at that moment, the Mallows in tow, and still a little mandarin in her embroidered coat.

"I found it in the bird book," explained Sophie. "It's great because it sounds so offensive."

Alan looked amused, and busied himself procuring mugs of coffee for mother and daughter. Sophie thanked him gratefully, while she wondered if she would have liked him quite so much if his name had been Ramsbottom.

Chapter 11

THE MILKING WAS DONE, THE UTENSILS WASHED and draining in the dairy. And Caroline, plunging arm deep into the frothy mess of the week's washing, ejaculated, "Good-bye, nailpolish! Though at least this is one way of getting your hands clean. The other being bread making."

"And I thought it was wholewheat," said Sophie sadly.

"I can't bear ironing because it only serves one purpose. Though I believe it's considered more genteel than washing. So you can do all the dashing away with the smoothing iron that you like."

"I don't mind, as long as I can listen to Jack Benny at the same time. But I do wish someone would tell me what 'corny' means. James says he doesn't know."

Sophie was making the inevitable picnic lunch, to take with her while road mending. The drive had become almost impassable, and she had decided to fill in the worst of the potholes.

"Banbury's say they won't be able to bring the delivery truck down if it gets much worse by the pond."

"Heigh ho for a surfeit of eggs if they stop collecting, and no shop food for us."

"Simplicity will be ready to leave her mother soon, Moya says. I hope she will like the eggs. Moya believes that puppies need raw eggs and milk, liver, cottage cheese, yeast, raw meat, cod-liver oil."

"More than we eat ourselves. And surely more words than you ever used to indulge in? Do you talk more, Sophie?"

"All good Canucks talk a lot, it's a national trait." She went off with her sandwiches, leaving her mother in the steamy cloud which was making her hair curl. Sophie had already rolled old denim overalls up to her knees, and had heavy brogues on her bare feet. Her hair, grown shoulder-length, was tied up in an orange-red scarf to keep out the dust of the chicken house, which she was going to clean before road making. She opened the door of the house where the hens were shut up nightly against the marauding coon and mink, and twenty-four New Hampshires flopped past her in a squawking mass. She filled their tins with laying mash and topped up the water, adding an old pot de chambre of skimmed milk to a different corner of the pen. She scattered wheat among the tufts of grass. Moscow watched over the gate of the chicken yard which kept her out; otherwise she would have eaten the hens' laying mash. Sophie used a broken-handled hoe to scrape off the dropping boards into a bucket, trying to hold her breath so that she wouldn't smell the disgusting, sweetish odour. But almost at once she said 'Good Morning' to some sleek damsel left inside, sitting on a nest, and who eyed her critically, the grey membrane over her small eyes drawn up in a bored and supercilious manner.

After emptying the bucket on the manure heap, she came back to collect the eggs. She was getting used to feeling under sitting hens and no longer recoiled from the sharp, snake-like jabs of their beaks on her arms and wrists. The eggs, cream, bronze, waxy brown, Easterish, had a fruitlike bloom, not one needing washing, they almost filled the basket.

This she left in the barn, well out of Moscow's reach, and whistling a cheerful but unrecognizable stave, then loaded up her barrow with spade and mattock, lunch and sweater, shut the yard gate, and trundled off up the hill. She kicked off bracken heads that had crooked through grass and plantains and clover, which grew like a ribbon up the middle of the road. Near the pond the ground was wet, and deep ruts made it almost impassable. The clatter of her approach suppressed the frog chorus. The mallard drake, on his own today, rose from the water, and with grace, upon his tilted wings, circled a couple of times before again alighting at the far end. The big grey crane, with his jaundiced face, also launched himself into the air, with maledictions, and trailing stiff yellow legs abandoned his meal of frog and went off to a fir tree.

Sophie sat herself down in the barrow with her legs extended stiffly, like the crane's, along each handle. A delightfully comfortable seat, she thought. From the bush she listened to the voice of what she knew to be a grouse, projected uneasily, stopping and starting, its direction uncertain, seeping through the thick undergrowth, or breathing down, even, from the treetops. She had already learned that many of the local creatures had this knack of throwing their voices — the blackfish who surfaced in schools to blow among the islands, making dolorous sounds from anywhere and everywhere, so that you always looked for them in the wrong direction. Even the frogs could now be perceived as twanging away, slightly out of tune, from all sorts of unexpected points. For at this time of year they seemed to spread themselves even on the road, little, jade green, or hazel and dark moss, their eyes gold pinpoints.

Reluctantly, she decided it was time to go to work, and heaved herself to her feet, with a last glance towards the pond to see if the crane had come back. The skunk-cabbage smell drifted back towards her, a wild arum which grew there. Most people hated it but she liked it. Its fleshy, lettuce-green leaves grew enormous, and shining with reflected light, looked quite good enough to eat for lunch. Rose said the Indians did use the boiled roots against consumption, and sometimes the leaves, too. The flowers were just coming out, a vivid, metallic yellow, very impressive. In the States, James said, they had learned how to de-odorize skunk cabbage and grew them in domestic rock gardens. But how sad thus to denature a plant so much a part of this scene.

She had better not even think about Alan until she had made progress with the road mending. He did, however, seem to accompany her like a shadow. Could some magical force have interchanged their shadows, so that he, too, was as curiously haunted by her? It had all happened so quietly, so naturally, for all the magic. She felt completely at home with him. She was as comfortable with him as with this island air.

As she pried up stones with her mattock, reluctantly tearing apart the thick moss which covered earth and fallen trees here, she bent to put each into her barrow, and then wheeled it off, tipping out the load, fitting each rock in its new place just as, she fondly thought, the Romans would once have done in Britain. Then she dug up sods and tramped them into the surrounding mud until there was a good, firm binding. James had shown her the proper procedure. Her hands suffered despite the heavy work gloves, and soon her back, too, ached. One more hole, further up the road, and she would permit herself lunch.

As she wheeled the heavy load, lurching through a puddle in order to avoid crushing daisies encrusting a turfy strip, she saw a shadow, and looked up to see the fish eagle rocking above her. He drew her eye towards a tall Douglas fir at the end of the drive, its trunk soaring branchless until it flung out into a mass of cones and needles. How tall could it be? In her mind's eye she always used the mental picture of her father as a measuring tape, because he had been exactly six foot tall. So now she wrapped him twice around the base of the huge tree, and then stood him end to end about fourteen times. Alan would have done as well, she suddenly realized, he too was six foot tall.

She could recognize a number of different trees all around — the cedar with its dark, crocheted edges hanging down shawl-like, the hemlock's fine hand-made lace displayed against the sky, the green and lacquered rosettes of arbutus and its lily-of-the-valley flowers, the grey, wool-work willow, with the worsted fluff of its seeds carried off by hummingbirds to line their nests, yellow-tasselled maples edged with moss, and the small cascara with its ridged leaves. She doted on them all, and gazed at them with endless satisfaction.

Disturbed by her rattling approach, a squirrel glared down over its shoulder from half-way up an oak tree, spread-eagled, beginning to yatter. It was a sparse grey-brown creature, rather ratlike, and with a tail less bushy than those she had known in England. Having filled the final hole, she tried unsuccessfully to level off a tree root breaking through the surface of the road. Then she ate her lunch and rested in the pleasant sun. A car was coming down the road.

Quickly she moved the barrow and tools, and Alan drove round the curve, slowing to a standstill as he saw her. He jumped out, carrying a bundle of mail, and they stood staring solemnly at each other.

"I hoped you would come."

"You're tired out!" he exclaimed, looking first at her face and then at the mattock. "Let me help."

She showed him the intractable tree root, and in no time he had hacked it away, and was wondering what else he could do.

"The days are too short. We never get time to do everything."

"They don't seem too short to me when you're not around. Come on, let's go down. Leave the wheelbarrow and I'll take you in the car."

He was thinking how even more attractive she looked today, in her working clothes, and streaked with mud, than she had last night in her fairy garb. He took her small, filthy, and capable hands and kissed them. He said, half astonished and with great tenderness, "There's mud on your face, Sophie, but you're lovely. Do you think we could possibly get married?"

She looked up at him, at the vermilion hair and the strong mouth, at his kind eyes and the sweetness of temper behind them, and at the comfort of him. "Oh yes," she smiled.

Caroline was in the kitchen washing sand out of the clumps of spinach. She cut the roots off carefully and saved them in a bowl of water, hoping that she would be able to plant them and thus get an early crop before the Noons. She looked quite often out of the window to admire her long strip of washing. But tall, dark clouds were piling up all of a sudden. She went outside with a basket to get the clothes in. It had been a busy day. Loath to waste the soapy water after the wash, she had first shampooed her own and Sophie's hairbrushes, and then scrubbed the kitchen table and floor.

Then she had milked early, and was filled with that sense of achievement which Moscow undoubtedly shared. She was waiting for Sophie to come back, listening for the trundling of the barrow as she collected the dry clothes from the line. But, back in the kitchen, finishing the spinach, she caught sight of her coming in with Alan, who bore the basket of eggs and letters.

"Hello Mr. Ramsbottom. Will you please both go back and wipe your feet again?" she gazed smugly at the floor.

"Oh Mum, you have been busy."

Caroline sighed a little, and then politely asked Alan if he would stay to supper.

"Surely, Mrs. Pomfret, I would love it. That is if you will let me peel that bowl of potatoes." He hung his jacket behind the door, and took the potatoes from an unprotesting Caroline. Sophie went off to the bathroom, having heard Alan mutter, "I'll tell her now."

"I am so happy," she thought to herself, though she wished the telling was over, and hoped it would be by the time she came back.

Caroline, unaware, sat smoking in her basket chair, happily regarding Mr. R's activities at the sink. In his primrose shirt which clashed quite attractively with his orange coloured hair, he looked both desirable and presentable, she thought — and how nice when the back of a man's neck was so attractive.

"There!" He put the potatoes in the water and added salt. "Shall I start cooking now?" His smile was distinctly nervous, and she wondered why, as she nodded.

He wandered towards her, drying his hands on the tea towel, and sat on the edge of the table. "Mrs. Pomfret, will you be my mother-in-law?"

Caroline stared at him stupidly. "This is of course some kind of joke. I don't know what you mean."

"No, no, it isn't a joke. Sophie and I want to get married. There hasn't been any time to tell you till now. I asked her this afternoon."

"But my good young man, Sophie isn't going to marry a Canadian — I mean, she isn't going to stay here, soon she's going back to where she belongs, to civilization."

Alan's greenish eyes narrowed but he said nothing.

"She's only eighteen," Caroline went on in a strangled voice, "and she thinks she knows enough about life to marry a man she's met a couple of times, and live with him happily ever after in the backwoods."

"You must have been as young when you married. And Sophie likes this country a lot. So do you really, except you're too restless to figure out what you're after. Sophie's wiser."

"Sophie's wiser!" she mimicked. "Your conceit is colossal, Mr. Ramsbottom. Wiser because you think she's in love with you, no doubt."

He laughed suddenly, throwing back his head and showing his good white teeth. And then the door opened and Sophie, wearing a spotless white shirt and shorts, peered round it, before coming in. She looked nervous but also radiant and fearfully young. Alan's laugh made her think all was well, so, before Caroline could begin to upbraid her, she enveloped her in a bear hug. "Aren't you glad, Mum? Isn't it marvelous? I'm so happy."

Caroline pulled herself free, but the remarks she had been going to make stayed unspoken. There was indeed such happiness in her daughter's usually tranquil face. All she could manage was one barbed comment. "He's told me. You poor besotted fool. But I suppose young love is never to be denied, much as I'd like to. Though you are not officially engaged, or any such stuff and nonsense, we will set a trial period of about five years and see what happens."

She went off to find the bottle of sherry, which had been Tim's reward for the use of her liquor permit. Poor Tim, poor Pierrot, she reflected, though to be honest she could not imagine Spens with that 'Tyger! Tyger! burning bright' look which was making Alan's expression so remarkable. Perhaps, after all, it was for the best. She certainly hoped so. That chit of a child! How had she, with her mother's instinct, not been aware? How had Sophie concealed, even for a week or two, this apparently devouring love for a Canadian shipwright whose name might or might not be Ramsbottom? Goodness, she had forgotten even to ask about his prospects. Well, she could remedy that right away. But just as she was going back, clutching bottle and glasses, a car drew up and Rose and James came hurrying in.

"Rose, dear, James. What news? Have you filed your petition yet? We're just going to have a sherry." She took them into the drawing-room and asked Alan, as if he was already one of the family, to light the fire, and sat them down. James, who looked more lined and rather puce, had hardly greeted her, or done more than mutter a response to her cheerful questioning.

"I'll break him for this!" he now exclaimed, accepting and gulping down his glass of sherry. "Mallow is sure he's heading for South America. He's taken her off, seized her. . . ."

"It's just another of Mallow's jokes," protested Rose, without great conviction, collapsing into the nearest chair.

"You look absolutely wan, Rose. Surely you can't be taking this ridiculous business seriously too?"

"Well, the trouble is, Tim is bound to get caught sooner or later. And if he's abducted Edna as well — James says it makes him look such a fool. He wouldn't let me go to the sewing circle this afternoon. And that will make even more talk. Everyone on the island is bound to be agog by now — poor Edna, carried off like that."

"Give them something to talk about," Caroline said callously.

"Oh Caroline! The police spent most of the morning asking us questions, they wouldn't leave until we promised to ring up if Edna manages to escape somehow, and find her way back. James says Tim will bring the boat in here, because the cove can't be overlooked, and he can feel fairly safe. Oh dear, I do wish it had been me and not Edna sleeping on board." Seeing Caroline smile, she suddenly looked less worried, and gave one of her old chuckles. "But really. Caroline you're the only person who can do a thing with Timothy. Why don't you marry him? If he ever comes back, that is?"

"Good God, what a monstrous idea. I'm far too old and infirm, and one new partnership in the family — infinitely deferred as it will be — is more than enough to be going on with."

Rose was too distracted to pick up the reference, and James continued to stare moodily at what was now a blazing fire. As his feet warmed up, he looked a little less enraged.

"After all's said and done, our Tim will find he's bitten off more than he can chew. Edna will be so angry, you can't imagine. She'll natter and natter, and he'll simply have to turn *Woodwind* around and bring her back. After all, the thing is, the police don't really have anything on him at all, and once he starts to think a bit, he'll realize that. I might bring a charge of abduction, of course, but that's probably something he won't think about."

"Now, now," said Rose soothingly, "don't keep dramatizing the situation, you're getting as bad as Tim. That's always been his trouble, he loves to feel in the thick of things, being chased and shot at, bootlegging. Quite harmlessly really — at least, until now." She stopped suddenly and listened. They all heard then a furtive, repeated triple knocking on the kitchen door."

"It's them!" shrieked Sophie and rushed out to open the door wide. All the others followed, in time to see Tim peering in, and asking, in a hoarse whisper, if the cops were there. Damp and dishevelled, he and Edna entered. Tim was laden with the box of china. Edna clung grimly to his elbow, pale and furious, tottered on her high heels.

"Here he is. Call the police, James." She snatched back her tea set and glared at her captor.

"Here she is, perfectly safe and sound, James. For God's sake, take her back. I'll gladly face all the police in the province. She's been — I can't describe how awful a time we've had. But do pull the curtains will you, dearest Caroline? Anyone can see in, they may be lurking out there, watching us."

"Tim, it's still daylight, don't be ridiculous. Anyway, you should be carrying Edna over the threshold, surely, rather than sounding so worn out and querulous."

Jim was tenderly removing his wife's wettish fur coat, but paused for a second to snarl, "Horse whipping's too good for him. If he won't be a man and give himself up I shall certainly call the police. Make up your mind, Spens, which course you prefer."

Tim unwound the muffler which concealed his face, and began to grin, "I didn't mean, for a second to go off with Edna. How could I know she was sleeping on my bunk? But if you only knew what else I had on board."

Edna, going out to the bathroom, stopped short on the stairs. "What did you have, beside me? I never saw a thing and I did look."

"Fortunately, my dear, you didn't wake up until I'd cached it. And since then you haven't stopped abusing me for long enough to listen. Really, Jim, I am most thankful to have brought her back to you."

Edna, still supported by James and Rose, went on, and the bathroom door banged. Tim threw himself into a chair and seized a double sherry which Caroline offered him. "What a relief to see your beautiful face and welcoming hands again. You're the real reason I came back to face the music, Caroline, instead of throwing Edna overboard and heading for South America."

Sophie, giggling, took Alan's hand, murmuring something about potatoes boiling dry and a need to see to other things in the kitchen.

"You mean, I suppose, that any port in a storm is desirable at this juncture of your sad affairs?"

"I mean that I have realized how impossible it is for me to live without you. Don't, please don't, ever desert me again, my dearest Caroline."

"Well," she said reflectively, "a good long relaxing cruise might be what we both need. Somewhere warm as the summer ends. I wonder if James and Edna would take on Moscow?"

Chapter 12

"TALKING ABOUT MARRIAGE," TIM BEGAN somewhat tentatively, a day or two later, and Caroline giggled.

"Sophie's in the cowshed, mucking out. We were so dreadfully late milking poor Moscow," she said.

"What on earth has that to do with marriage?" asked Tim.

"Another part of life, that's all. I might as well ask why you wanted to talk about marriage, though it is not an unsatisfactory aspect of life, when one thinks about it."

Tim brightened. "Good. I was afraid you had made up your mind not to think about it."

"The dream I had last night started me off. I've often had it lately. Perhaps it's a premonition of death."

"Caroline!"

"To be honest, James began it all, with his fireside chats about funeral homes, and then that awful fancy dress affair. I see myself laid out in a velvet draped casket, in my black lace negligee, my hands and face small and white like lilies. Beside me, weeping among clusters of tea roses, kneels Sophie, orphaned to a strange land. Then tears start from under my dead eyelids in sympathy, and form little pools of wax on the pillow." She sniffed and blinked, moved by the vision and her recital of it.

Spens produced a handkerchief, which he first unfurled and then solicitously handed to her. He took up the theme.

"Your hair, freshly finger-waved, gives back the candlelight. How strange, how remote but beautiful you look, like a Dante Gabriel Rossetti. I stand in the shadows inside the half-open door, my head is bowed with grief. The candles flutter. I am unable to repress admiration for the swell job the morticians have done on you, 'A tisket, a tasket, Carrie in her casket.' "

Caroline returned her handkerchief rather pettishly. "I suppose I have a hangover once again," she said. "That's the trouble with your visits to the cove, we cannot resist your wares."

Sophie's voice broke in with a startling suddenness, from the hall above the drawingroom. "Come in Mrs. Stanway. If you don't mind, I'll just take off my Wellingtons on the mat. Moscow, you know."

Caroline made a face, and Tim whispered, "They've come to excommunicate us," as she went out.

"How much nicer are Wellingtons than gumboots," rumbled Mr. Stanway's voice, "Why ever did we drop that lovely term?" That was generally taken as one of his rhetorical questions, which no one need much notice. The visitors were brought in, and Mrs. Stanway, rather handsome in a faintly clerical way, admired the new arrangements of the big room, while apologising for her failure to have visited before. She and Caroline stood at one of the long windows and tried to discover the view through rain, now falling in swathes, blotting out mountains and blurring even the nearest islands. The oily sea, freckled with its drops, sucked at the dark, uncovered rocks. A tug slid by, towing a shadowy log boom, and quickly vanished. The turf on the point, close cropped by Moscow, glowed synthetic green among arbutus trunks which gleamed as if lacquered in the downpour.

"They are wearing their nylons," said Caroline.

"Because they are so silky?" Mrs. Stanway nodded sympathetically. "But they are so dreadfully untidy, aren't they? They go shedding their leaves all summer, and their skin peels off. Not my ideal of a garden tree. Over there, if we could only see it, is the island where the Doukhobors were imprisoned, poor things. I don't suppose you knew that."

Sophie and Tim made a fortunate diversion by getting an early tea. The centrepiece was a chocolate cake, a well-timed present from Tim, who explained that the dance club committee always waxed fat on leftover trifles of this sort.

"I am so fond of chocolate cake, moist like this one, fragrant with vanilla," said Mr. Stanway, actually licking his lips.

"And peppermint icing?" Tim suggested.

"Indeed, though peppermint essence is still hard to come by, we are regularly told. Where does it hail from, Mrs. Pomfret?"

"Sophie, fetch the encyclopedia. It's a truly venerable copy, but that, at least, ought to be included."

"Mint," read out the Vicar a minute later. " An odiferous plant yielding a pungent, essential oil."

"How beautiful!" breathed Timothy.

"And also," the Vicar went on, cocking an eyebrow at him, "a place of invention or fabrication. Perhaps even a still, though it is too polite a book to say so."

Mrs. Stanway hastily intervened. "You must at least get all the butter and cream you need now, with your new cow."

"So much so that we hardly feel it is worth milking her again. This morning we gave her a little much-needed peace, she's only just been done, and that must last till tomorrow."

"Good gracious!" exclaimed Mrs. Stanway. "Our Molly wouldn't stand for such treatment."

"What could she do about it?"

"She'd moo all through matins," Tim answered for him. "She once did, when they failed to milk her. I was there, and felt quite shattered when she took up the strains of 'Abide With Me'. Mallow said afterwards he had simply thought it was Edna in particularly good voice, but then he is notoriously tone deaf. Since then I have felt it wiser to observe Sabbath listening to the concert hour on the wireless. Though even that begins to pall. Snippets of Smetana, and *Peter and the Wolf* every other week. It has become a sort of musical *Reader's Digest*."

"Digest for readers, a magazine digest, a digest of the news, the heart of the symphony, the kidneys of the concerto, all so symptomatic of our culture's spoon-feeding," the vicar sadly agreed.

"I must say, though, I do enjoy the *Reader's Digest*," his wife mildly put in. "It is such a help in conversation. Everyone knows the source of what you say, naturally, but in a way, that helps in discussion."

Spens smiled, and held out his cup to be re-filled. "Caroline, you need only a corsage to look the picture of Mom, presiding over the tea urn. Mrs. Pomfret, graciously filling teacups at a local baby shower."

" 'Mom!' " She banged down the teapot. "That's another thing about this continent, it absolutely obsessed with 'Mom.' It's practically the heart of 'Mom,' isn't it? I had someone on the wireless yesterday assuring us 'Mom's' home cooking was what the boys had really been fighting for. As if her apple pie were some sort of universal panacea, a symbol of democracy."

Sophie exploded with laughter. "Dear 'Mom,' no one would fight for your apple pie, so take comfort. Pastry isn't my 'Mom's' strong point," she explained.

"I suppose you refer to my apple tart? What ingratitude. Talk about serpent's teeth."

"I cannot help agreeing with you," said Mr. Stanway, smiling, "that the instincts of motherhood have been exploited in this deplorably materialistic and strongly sentimental land. On every Mother's Day one is forced, shame-faced, into buying a fur coat, or at least a pot plant, for the loved figure. Even Father, when his day comes, can hope for a pair of socks. His family knows that if this is not forthcoming he will grow embittered and sulk. Mine club together and buy me a nicely embellished card."

Tim had grown tired of a conversation others had taken over, and was trying to get the fire to burn better, using a leaky pair of bellows. A few woodlice appeared, and he lifted them tenderly and dropped them in to a nearby bowl of daffodils. "So defenceless. They haven't even learned to curl up properly into balls like their European cousins. They have no 'Mom' to teach them. But Sophie, you really should stack up the firewood to dry. It can't be expected to burn if it comes straight out of the sea."

"Something else their mums haven't taught the European cousins?" Sophie scowled at him before resuming her conversation with Mrs. Stanway — mostly on the subject of the clerical twins, now being described as fervent admirers of her.

"Really, there's simply too much to do," interposed Caroline, wearily. "Just keeping going seems to take all our time and energy."

"Precisely. That's why you should be living on a boat."

"But one would miss a garden," said Mrs. Stanway.

"Not any more," Caroline answered with feeling.

"Besides, you can plant dear little gardens on very unpeopled islands. I remember poking in some cos lettuce seeds one year, but I've never been able to remember which island. I used to go round and round searching hungrily."

"How touching," responded Sophie. "The next time Tim disappears in *Woodwind*, I shall picture him on a radish hunt, or bedding out geraniums by the wild seawaves."

"My child, you sound acerbic," he said hastily, to drown out Mr. Stanways's clear intention of using this opportunity to enquire once more about the most recent disappearance. Caroline took her cue, and between them they talked so much that the visitors soon got up to leave, their curiosity unassuaged.

Tim at once asked if he might take a hot shower before he went back to *Woodwind* — so much simpler to make one's toilet ashore, specially as the water was so gloriously hot.

"Of course. Even a long hot bath, if you prefer."

"I prefer showers, they brace me up instead of relaxing me into supinity."

"Ah, like Blake I say, 'Damn braces, bless relaxes.' "

Moya had casually told Sophie weeks ago that Tim always liked to make free of his friends' bathrooms, and Sophie had been waiting for this moment ever since. For she had discovered that if she suddenly turned on the hot tap in the kitchen, the flow to the shower was cut off. Instead of a judicious mixture, balmy, soothing, one was dreadfully assailed by a sharp and icy deluge. And the same in reverse — as her mama would have said, "The morning like the lobster boiled, from black to red began to turn." She had been longing to work this trick on Tim, who increasingly seemed to her selfish and egotistic. After alarming poor Rose and James so, he would now get what was coming to him.

So she listened carefully, waiting in the kitchen. He had begun to warble happily, sure token of immersion in delightful, warm water. "How happy I could be with either," his tenor voice maintained. She let him finish the verse and rapidly turned the hot tap on as fast as it would run. A pitiable shriek came from above followed by an even louder one as she turned it off, and turned on the cold.

Caroline rushed in, looking positively alarmed, to find her daughter convulsed with laughter. She could not speak for quite a minute, and then, still groaning, she explained the joke.

"Oh, poor Tim! I thought he must be having a fit, I was just nerving myself to go in and save him. You naughty child, why didn't you tell me the trick before?"

"I was afraid you wouldn't be able to resist trying it out on poor James. Or even on me. Do you suppose Aunt Mary knew about it?"

"She was far too godly to do it, I'm sure. Though maybe someone did it to her. What a whale of an idea for a murder story. I shall sell it to Hollywood, Sophie. Think of Jack Benny in just such a trick shower! We will make heaps of money and be able to go back to Europe."

"I don't want to go back," Sophie said stiffly.

"Oh, what a dreary life you are bent on leading. And what do you think I shall do if you really insist on marrying Mr. Ramsbottom? Live on here all alone, milking the cow with my increasingly rheumatic fingers?"

"You'd better marry Tim. I'm sure you would be good for him, and he might even be good for you."

Chapter 13

IT SEEMED TO HAVE BEEN DECIDED by everyone that she and Tim would suit each other, Caroline meditated, as she lay sunbathing, really sunbathing for the first time, upon their small white beach. How curious. But was it really a possibility? Tim certainly thought it was, and Rose, and now Sophie. But then Sophie must be feeling guilt-ridden, anything to dispose of Mum in a graceful fashion. She did not know that she had been destined for Tim. She would have mocked the idea uproariously. Wasn't it Tim that Sophie was to marry?

"Too, too technicolour!" reflected Caroline — not about her scheming gone astray, but about the deep blue sky, cloudless, filtering through the slightly waving banners of the maple which overhung the end of the cove. Perhaps her sunglasses, which were the only thing she wore, gave it an added splendour, but she felt too indolent to take them off and find out. She would never have supposed it could be hot enough here to swoon away such an idle afternoon, for the sea, naturally, for all its gem-like clarity, was still impossibly frigid — much too cold ever to warm up — whatever happened to flaming summer? Sophie had gone off with Ramsbottom and a party of energetic young friends, setting off almost at dawn in his boat to explore the islands.

What seas, what shores,
What grey rocks and what islands,
What water lapping the bow,
What images return O my daughter.

Just as long as the daughter did return. No eloping in that dreadful Tim fashion, abducted females screaming and clutching their household goods. She dozed, woke to see a silver TCA plane passing far too high to see her, then a hummingbird flashing by, making small wheels of light with its pulsating wings, a jewelry bird, hanging like a falcon, or a helicopter, darting in the swiftest dive to perch on a twig, flame and peacock sheen of feathers visible now, body as big as her thumb nail, long delicate beak thrusting after honey. Suddenly, with an almost bat-like squeak, it flew straight up into heaven. She turned over to brown a different part, and could then see the black skullcap of her familiar seal in the bay, disappearing every moment without a ripple to fish among the kelp roots.

Ramsbottom's prospects were, in fact, quite good. He owned a remunerative and not ungentlemanly business, his mother was charming — quite able, when they had met, to deal with Caroline's dubious enquiries. And so, after all, only two months after she had practically forbidden the engagement, she found herself agreeing to the insertion next week of a notice in the wedding column of *The Daily Colonist*. Now Tim was planning a kind of picnic reception for the Happy Couple on *Woodwind*, while Alan had tentatively formed his tongue around the title of 'Mama'. She had decided that she would give Arbutus Point as a post-dated wedding present. It was near enough to Fulford Harbour for Alan to commute, and Sophie would not have to leave the place she loved more each day. All that was left was to plan her own future. She would have to make up her mind now, while Tim was away in Vancouver.

He had offered to sail Mrs. Graham back there, declaring that the sight of Sophie and Alan, walking hand in hand everywhere, in the broadest daylight, was too much for him. He felt both queasy and envious.

And when he came back, a couple of days later, he was to bring a mess of fresh oolichans from the Fraser River, upon which they would dine. Caroline was not sure that she much looked forward to that tiny fish loved by the Indians, who had kept them for months in tubs and used the oil, which smelled, for lamp fuel. She'd even heard that they were so richly oily that if you lit the tail of one it would burn like a wick. After getting tired of eating them, Tim cooked them like fresh whitebait, which she did enjoy, so perhaps they would be alright. He would bring brown bread to eat with them and she was to provide lots of young asparagus from the old bed in her garden, and a tipsy cake. But she hoped he would bring some cheese, too — impossible to get anything worth eating here for the last few weeks. And perhaps he would remember coffee. And booze, of course. She was growing rather to rely on Tim.

Absent-mindedly she started to make herself a sea garden in the million, million particles of the clamshell beach, disturbing sand fleas who leapt up like explosive bubbles. Here, at her age, and on this alien beach, she was using the same technique as in her childhood on a colder, greyer, more boisterously windswept shore. One swept the sand smooth with the edge of the hand, thus constructing low enclosing walls; then, with only a fingertip, one made circular garden beds, which one planted with anything to hand. One built a shell grotto, overhung by a stunted pine of dry seaweed, a shell pool, with its banks fashioned of pebbled rockeries and strips of green seaweed made grassy paths. She could even smell the sour aroma of that bathing tent, to the shelter of which you ran from cold, turbulent dips across the endlessly wretched gale-whipped pebble and sand beach.

She remembered the excruciating rubbings-down there, during which you screamed and whimpered, as sand ground into your tender, blue flesh, perhaps already a little pink from some stray shafts of sunlight and therefore even sorer.

Then you put on that white cricket sweater with its wide collar, and were given a chunk of fruitcake too dry to be enjoyable but better than nothing for the chattering teeth to clench upon. Or that terrible thing, a marmalade sandwich. How had one ever survived such a holiday? One thing was, it seldom actually rained. Probably the gales had prevented it. Though there were some even more uncomfortable hours, when they had all been fretful and quarrelsome, having to consume tea crouched among deckchairs in the smelly bathing tent, sand creeping into the aptly named sandwiches, milk curdled in a lime juice bottle and sour oranges which were sucked through a lump of sugar. It all came back, bit by bit — Nanny's irritated voice across so many years, as clear as if it had been recorded: 'Don't touch the tent, Miss Caroline — now don't. The rain will come through and soak us all.' Even the earwigs. For earwigs there had been, sharing the flimsy shelter, offering each time the welcome opportunity for one of them to shriek, 'Ear-wego — that's what he said as he slid down the tent pole!'

Happy days, rather than unhappy. Enormous holes excavated until water level was finally reached, the making of a mummy if anyone could be persuaded to lie still long enough, hands crossed on bosom, all to be coated with damp sand, even, sometimes, the face, though eyes and mouth had to be excepted, and sand always did get in, and the rows and scenes and reproaches from that almost always reproachful Nanny.

Lucky Sophie had Ramsbottom, no nanny for them, or their luckier children. She could feel now, as she hung over her abandoned garden, the heavy weight of a spadeful of wet sand dumped upon her warm tummy.

She had had to learn a hymn for punishment, perhaps for filling with sand the eyes and mouth of one of the others. She had sat on what she now remembered as hot purple shingle, which felt quite greasy to the touch, and worked away at it. It had added to the joy of living in that day's world of shimmering sunshine, enthusiastic wind, acres of hard crimped sand which was rippled and edged in the mould of the departed tide. She had run and run, leaping blue drainage channels, chanting 'Hail to the Lord's Anointed,' to some abandoned, straw-filled palliasses, to razor shells and starfish, and bunched seaweed which she kept trying to eat, surprised each time by its grittiness. She had been the Lord's Anointed, she had been the essence of that remarkable, seaside day.

She shook herself, got up, washed in a small, warm rock-pool, and put on her clothes. The intrusion of all those memories, as if through the flimsiest partition walls, into this totally different time and place, had disturbed her. She would leave the beach, go and walk around the apple orchard, where there seemed always to be a lingering scent of honey, long after the pink and white blossoms had yielded to dwarfish, incipient apples, a crop she was beginning to count upon to help cover such expenses as a new dress and hat for the wedding.

Big rusty Canadian robins scattered at her approach, calling loudly. A flock of red-winged woodpeckers, called 'flickers', who had been feeding in the grass instead of doing as they should and laboriously hammering their meals out of the tree trunks, also rose. Alan, who went on what were oddly described as birding expeditions, had told them of the interest aroused in his companion voyeurs by this decadent mutation.

A hummingbird flashed among these trees, too, and suddenly, at eye level and only two yards away, she met the unflinching stare of a tiny mother, sitting tight on her egg cup of a nest, which Caroline could see was wonderfully formed of mosses and lichens and fluff from the nearby Balm of Gilead Tree. She could not stop gazing at this heavenly vision, but did at last back away, fearful of terrifying that indomitable small mother who would, clearly, rather break her neck or her heart than desert her young. When Tim came back she must bring him, on tiptoe, to look. She knew he would enjoy it in much the same way as herself.

Chapter 14

SOPHIE AND ROSE WERE SPENDING twenty-four hours together while Edna and James, for a change of scene, had gone to stay with Caroline. It was a good opportunity, before Mavis came into milk again, with the imminent birth of her calf. James would milk Moscow, Caroline would cook a ravishing dinner, Edna could sit in the sun and crochet.

But Rose and Sophie were going immediately into the bush which divided the two properties, to cut cascara bark and make some money. They each had a sharp knife, and Rose demonstrated the knack of employing them. You made an incision in the dappled grey bark horizontally, and then cut two long vertical lines, about two to three inches apart, before carefully lifting the loosened strip from the tree. The wet bark smelt refreshingly astringent and looked damp yellow. This didn't kill the tree, she assured an anxious Sophie. Later on, she said, it would be cut down at the level where the bark had been stripped, and simply shoot up again.

They worked hard and almost in silence, until they had filled their two sacks. These they carried back to spread out near the house where the bark could dry in the sun. It might not sell for much, but it was always in demand, and it was a standard means of living off the land.

"They're always talking about establishing a mill to deal with it," Rose continued, in her steady and sequential way, to illuminate Sophie's ignorance of the BC economy. "It would make use of whole branches then, putting them through a crushing machine, extracting lots of juice. Let's not do any more now, it's getting so hot, and the flies and mosquitoes will be even worse in the bush. Let's go over to the old reserve for a swim."

Sophie accepted with delight, having brought her bathing dress in just such a hope. As they walked, slowly and companionably, Rose pointed out slight mounds where once had been Indian buildings. They could see the occasional, plant-covered timber cross-beams, which had roofed over houses and canoe shelters. There was a stream which they crossed by jumping from one rock to another, a pile of stones where a fireplace had once smoked, the swell of an old midden, the fallen supports of a dock. Rose's mind was full of the old times, she wanted Sophie, too, to know about them, to inherit, in some tenuous way, anecdotes which no one else cared to remember. This land did have a history, the trouble was it was unwritten. The unlettered ghosts of millennia of Indians were pushed out of consciousness by crude incoming whites, just because they could not hear or see that past.

"There used to be a medicine man and his wife here even when we first built our house. Very old and wonderfully self-reliant. They had some money which they always kept in bills in their shoes. Everyone knew it. But one night they came back from a visit to an island and were set upon before they could beach the canoe. They were murdered and robbed. No one ever found the bodies, only the upturned canoe, floating a long way out. But the dreadful screams were heard across the water, though none of us could get there very quickly through the dark and rain. We found the shack half demolished — the murderer must have been ransacking it in the hope of more money."

"Didn't they ever find out who had done it?"

"No. But that's one reason the Indians never came here anymore. It's unlucky. For them, at least."

"It doesn't feel sinister, does it? I'm glad you brought me, and told me the tragic story. Do you suppose this fireplace was the medicine man's?"

"It's so hard to remember after all these years. Perhaps it was nearer the sea — those timbers were the community house, I do know. If you dig around in the midden, you might even find some old tools."

Sophie began at once, using her bare hands, and actually, after a busy ten minutes, came upon what looked like a chipped black spearhead, which they both gleefully examined and exclaimed over. Like two schoolgirls they hurried to climb the rocks, coming at last onto a clifftop, where they slithered dangerously on bleached arbutus leaves which had drifted everywhere, so brittle that they splintered underfoot. They sniffed the aromatic air, which Caroline always compared to the south of France, Sophie said. And then they slid down to another beach. Grey pebbles sloped there into the quite deep water, and there was a grassy platform where logs must have been rolled out. This beach was shaded by giant, moss-coated maples, and the mountains looming over it were silent with their burden of regrown forest. They filled the can they had brought with water at the well where the remains of a lean-to still stood and exclaimed at the number of deer slots in the mud around.

Rose had a beach fire permit, so they gathered wood, lit a fire, and went to swim while it heated. The sea was indeed bitingly cold, but that did not spoil their intense pleasure as they plunged into its clear bright green. Sophie splashed Rose, who splashed back in a desultory way before she hurried ashore. Sophie then swam very energetically indeed, to stop the paralysis she felt creeping though her.

By the time she had dried, the water had boiled, and Rose was making tea to drink with their hard-boiled eggs and crisp salad of her own lettuce, radishes and spring onions. She had also made the nice brown bread which Sophie was consuming so much of.

They lay for a while, in happy, companionable silence again, too full of contentment to move or speak. Then it was time to extinguish every spark and ember of the fire, to make sure that their cigarette butts were also safely out, and to set off for home. They filled the water can with late wild strawberries as they made their way across the clearings.

Here crickets chirped among the ripe grasses, above rocks whose lichen coverlets were brittle and faded. From the dry moss grew many purple and papery flowers, and white and mauve flowering balls of wild onion. Yellow daisies and stone crop pushed from crevices hanging over the sapphire water. They walked knee-deep through beds of pale, purplish rock flowers, and then caught sight of some exquisite yellow ones, which Rose insisted were musk, but which Sophie privately believed to be calceolaria. They passed into a silent spruce wood where there was no underbrush, and even the overgrown track was suddenly distinct. A bleached pile of sheep bones gleamed in the twilight as a quail called. They pushed, relieved, through a final canopy of branches and a wall of green bracken, out again into the dazzle and glare of sunlight and sea. Rose showed Sophie some horrid grey bags where, here and there, a creature known as the Tent Caterpillar was beginning to destroy old fruit trees, survivors from older times, bearded with moss. The infesting caterpillars would eat every leaf. Soon these trees, like so many elsewhere, would be killed.

You had to take down each sticky bag, oozing with its striped yellow and grey young, and burn them or perhaps squelch them underfoot. Sophie shuddered at the thought, but Rose told her seriously that this was what each one of the islanders must do, for only the lady-bird was natural enemy to this plague of devourers, who spared only evergreens, and, strangely, pear trees.

But quite suddenly, Sophie stopped listening. On the nearby island, she caught sight of Alan's shack, and her thoughts sped across the water, she could think of nothing else. "Rose," she said, "I know Mother wouldn't mind. She's agreed to an announcement in the paper next week, but I want you to know first. Alan and I are engaged, we're going to get married quite soon. As soon as we can persuade her to the next step."

"Oh, my dear!" Rose stooped, hugged Sophie, and wiped away a tear. "Oh, how wonderful! That means you won't go away, you'll stay here and be one of us. I can't tell you how sad I've felt every time your mother talks about taking you back home."

"I love it here. Even if it wasn't for Alan I'd stay, surely you must have felt that?"

"In a way. But then you are so young. Still, old enough to get married, it seems. Why don't we ring him up as soon as we get home, and ask him to supper? He won't have left yet. That is, if you think he won't mind fish pie? I made it last night, and it's got shrimps and lots of egg in it."

"It sounds wonderful."

"And you can pick garden strawberries to eat with these and we have cream. And even a bit of mousetrap Edna managed to buy yesterday."

"It will be a feast. Darling Rose, you are so kind to me."

Alan, naturally, leapt at the invitation. He would have eaten stale, unbuttered bread in order to share it with Sophie. But he was not too besotted to notice how excellent was the supper Rose prepared. The three of them had a happy time, vying with each other to see who could come up with the newest or most striking Canadian idiom. There was no need to be polite or to offer each other second helpings. They reached for whatever they fancied, they guffawed at each other's jokes.

After clearing up, Rose suggested further celebration, knowing quite well that she would never have dared if Edna had been at home. Why didn't they go to the beer parlour and toast, in real liquor, a future happiness?

"It could be a little rough, Rose. Because of the walk-out, you know," responded Alan with unusual prudence. "Perhaps we should wait till another night."

"But we know them all, they're our friends." Rose brushed aside his hesitation. "Don't start to get middle-aged already. You and Sophie must enjoy your glorious youth."

Sophie had forgotten that the woodworkers were going on strike, and that this was the first day. She had heard it talked about for weeks, but somehow she could not remember anything except her joy. That was why, she suddenly realized, the walk across the Indian Village had been so very silent — no sounds of logging from across the mountain, no dragsaw and whistle punk. All the booming grounds must be deserted, there would have been no logs, today, hurtling from the great trucks down into the water, sending up their markers of white splashing.

Alan did not long have to be persuaded, and the three of them squeezed into the front seat of his car, and drove off, still giggling at each other's feeble jokes, to celebrate. It was already quite late when they arrived, making towards the head of the inlet, where the lights of the little beer parlour twinkled in a deceptively cosy manner across the water. Its garden of flowering bushes and marigolds was glowing with faint, last evening light, but a mass of parked cars and trucks contradicted such pastoral charm, as did the shouting and raucous laughter that assaulted them when they went in.

The room did have a slightly pub-like and English appearance, Sophie thought, though perhaps more like those newish brewery places built on a by-pass somewhere. The cigarette smoke smelt quite different, and the bar was right up at the far end and curiously uncrowded, when at home it would have been six-deep with customers. Alan explained to her, after a tough-looking character wearing a green eyeshade and a windbreaker had come up to take their order, that it was illegal here to drink at the bar, or, indeed, to play any musical instrument. Barmaids were not allowed, hence the male "beverage dispenser," and you couldn't have anything except beer, not even a sandwich to eat with it.

"It doesn't stop them drinking, though," Rose observed rather tartly. "He has to whiz around the tables, doesn't he?"

Sophie, watching the tough guy, now joined by his boss, fetching more and more glasses, until the tables were packed solid, could not but agree. She felt a little ill-at-ease here, and reached for Alan's hand under the table.

Then someone he knew came over, and said hello to the three of them, adding that there had just been a wedding, and pointing out the bridesmaids over in the corner. Charming young things they looked, in their wreaths and veils and gowns of pink and blue, but the gowns were stained with beer, and the girls peered in a cock-eyed way from under the tulle and rosebuds. Their escorts looked even worse for wear, and were bellowing out snatches of song and unappealing laughter.

"Is that why you were worrying, Alan? That people who are not respectable come here?"

He laughed. "They have the most respectable parents you can imagine, and come from Ganges. But people do drink too much when they come here, no getting away from it."

The man in the eyeshade rushed up to ask if they were ready for another beer, but Alan shook his head, and they slowly sipped at what they had. Rose got up to visit with a party of people near by. They looked happy to see her, their teeth flashing welcoming smiles like summer lightning. These were the descendants of those runaway slaves she'd heard about, as Alan whispered to her. They lived at the north end of the island, and were kind, prosperous folk. One of them, old, old, maybe more than a hundred, had recently died in the hospital. She used to relate wonderful stories, which had been told her as a child, about the arrival on the island, when the Indians and they had fought in the thick bush by the beaches. Later they had been granted land to settle on, and had flourished without many problems ever since.

The din increased steadily, Sophie could hardly hear what Alan was saying. They made gestures at each other, smiled, held hands more openly. Rose came back and said she'd like another beer, please, they hadn't properly toasted future matrimony and happiness. She seemed oblivious of the sinister-faced men standing around, talking to each other from the sides of their mouths, so that Sophie asked Alan if they packed guns. Outside someone was noisily vomiting, inside a man shouted the ugly word "Scab!" Alan looked around quickly, but the moment passed. A couple of men in checked mackinaws and pale blue, peaked cotton caps, moved closer to their table, and Sophie was relieved to find they were friends.

"Howya' making out?" Alan asked them.

"Shut down, like everyone else. It's going to be real tough."

"We'll have to be slowing down if it lasts. But at least our lumber is seasoned and we've got a great supply. So I could give you two fellas a job for the next two weeks," Alan said.

They started to look much happier, and agreed to come down to the yard the next day and see about it. Meanwhile, how about a beer for him and the two ladies?

Then the lights went out, and a glass smashed to the floor. A groan and a boo went up, the tension felt as tangible as a taut rubber band. Alan pulled Sophie and Rose to their feet just as the light came on again. He and his two friends walked them over the door in a silent, solid phalanx, safely out, and over to the car. "It's only the strike," one of the men said, apologetically. "It isn't always like that, tell your girlfriend."

The night smelled fresh, the strong scent of the mud flats refreshing. The searchlight of a police boat flashed on the water, the second man said with a laugh that it must be the new sergeant, moving around, ready for mischief. They all said goodnight, and Alan carefully drove them home, loitering a little in the garden with Sophie, while Rose pretended to bed Mavis down.

"Sophie, I've got you a ring. Look!" He slipped a half loop of diamonds onto her finger and then kissed it. "Better not wear it till after the notice comes out though."

"Oh, lovely, lovely! It shines like phosphorous in seawater. Thank you, dearest Alan. I'm so happy."

Chapter 15

ROSE FELT AS IF SHE HAD BEEN COOKING for weeks. Tim was giving his party in honour of Sophie's engagement that night — and it also just happened to be his birthday. So dozens of people were coming, there was no end to what they would consume.

He had airily handed over all the catering arrangements to Rose, who decided that they must have a sort of smorgasbord. Now, excited, nervous, but supremely happy, she started to check over all that had been done, all that still needed doing.

Jellied chickens glistened in the cooler, cracked crabs were waiting to be assembled into a salad. A neighbouring islander had smoked both salmon and tongue — not synthetically, painting on some meretricious substance, but properly, slowly, in the real alder wood smoke of his own, chimney-like smoke house. There were regiments of gherkins, Himalayas of crisp red cabbage, navy beans, pickled herrings from her own storeroom. All the previous day she had been making and baking, and dark rye bread was carefully packed up next to trays of minute and fascinating sausage rolls.

A rather flushed Edna vigorously beat mayonnaise at the kitchen table. For Moya had found a bottle of real olive oil among the ARP supplies, and had thoughtfully sent it along, together with anchovies and liver sausage procured by Mallow in Victoria.

"It is lucky that my hens are laying so well," she said, glancing from the mayonnaise just beginning to cling to the whisk to the heap of hard-boiled eggs beside it and complacently licking her fingers.

"Do go slow on the finger licking," said Rose a little sharply. "You know there isn't a drop more oil. It's just as well Tim is going to bring a few extras from Vancouver — though when one thinks that half the world is actually starving, it does seem perfectly dreadful. I suppose he will remember? And Edna, do you think Caroline will remember to bring the cream and canned asparagus?"

"She may. I doubt it, though."

"Oh, she will, I'm sure she will. Now, chicken livers, and where are those precious olives? I mustn't forget the paper napkins. Will you say 'paper napkins' to me in half-an-hour?" And she deftly removed the platter of sausage rolls from her sister-in-law's reach, just as James strode in with a basket of green stuff. "Horns of plenty!" he exclaimed, looking around before he dumped his contribution in the butler's pantry. "What's for elevenses, Rose?"

"A little of the patty on rye bread, and some coffee?" she suggested, pushing up her glasses and smiling at her brother.

"Who is giving this party?" he asked, peering into the congested cooler. "I thought it was Tim, but it looks more like us."

"Well, we're doing all the work, as usual," grumbled Edna.

"Tim is providing drinks, coffee, ice cream, and smokes," Rose said palliatively. "Don't you wish we could live off this sort of food all summer?"

"Good idea. Saves washing up, too. You could eat everything off one plate. Or even just off a canapé." He gulped his coffee, and pushed back the cup for more. "After all, at least that's something from Tim."

"It is his birthday, don't forget."

"We won't be allowed to. And really, we're all going just because it's Sophie's engagement party."

"Yes," Edna agreed, "I certainly would never set foot on that boat again for any other reason."

"Everyone is so pleased about it," James went on. "Myself, I don't know which of them is the luckier, Sophie or Alan. Caroline was saying she had really wanted it to be Spens, though she's now quite resigned. He's far too old, don't you think?"

Edna laughed heartily. "Timothy Spens of all people! If only she knew — but he'll get his just deserts one of these days, mark my words."

"Though meanwhile he seems to be getting ours," James said sadly. "Did you make that marvellous cake, Rose?"

"Oh no. The rector's mother made it, and they brought it first thing this morning. And one of his wife's famous soups."

"All I hope is that he gets back in time for the party. We can't decently have it without him, I suppose."

"Good gracious," Rose panicked, "what shall we ever do with all this food if he doesn't?"

"We could have a party OK, but there wouldn't be any drink. He's got all our ration cards for the month on board."

"You are so foolhardy," said Edna. "Just suppose you get caught trading liquor books — we'd all end up in jail. A nice thing that would be. What would your family back home say? James, do fill the sawdust hopper, now you're here. Then we can cook ourselves a little something for lunch — not that I'm the slightest bit hungry. In fact, I feel almost nauseated at the sight of so much food. I do want to have a little rest afterwards, I'm completely worn out." She licked a succulent glob of mayonnaise off her finger.

* * * *

Rose changed rapidly into a sprigged cotton dress, which she wore with her own angular kind of grace, while Jim and Edna were still decking themselves out for the party. *Woodwind's* engines, thank the Lord, could by now be heard approaching, and very soon Tim was rowing ashore, looking smart enough for Cowes in his white flannels, dark blazer and yachting cap.

Rose turned him round and round in order to inspect him better. "There, but you're beautiful when you're all shined up! A happy birthday, dear Tim — here's a small something from me." She produced a parcel wonderfully done up in tissue paper and tinselled ribbon she had borrowed from the Christmas box.

"Oh, tribute!" he exclaimed, kissing her warmly and at once untying all the knots with clever fingers, as she perched on a chair arm and eagerly watched, at least as anxious as he to see what was inside. She had been, now and again, romantically in love with him. But most of the time he seemed more like her child, even though they were about the same age. She was sure that he knew all her feelings and exploited them to the utmost — though in a nice way, of course.

"You are my real family, dearest Rose," he exclaimed in delight, as he drew out a pair of sheepskin mules which she had bought for him after the fancy dress dance when his poor feet had looked so cold and blue. "Look, I've got something for you, too."

He brought out of his pocket a small, neat package. "Open it now, before anyone else comes. It's a little something for the chef." Delighted, flushed, she looked much younger, he thought, almost adolescent, half his own age, anyway. She fingered the slim silver cigarette case, lying amongst its cushion of cotton wool, with a look of surprise and reverence.

"But Tim, this can't be for me."

"If you cry I shall give it to Edna," he said severely. "Then she'll be quite sure I've always had designs on her, and planned that entire abduction. So will Mouseykins."

James looked anxiously around the door just then so all she could do was hug Tim, and put the marvellous case — filled, she later discovered, with cigarettes — into her handbag.

"Thank goodness you've got here, Tim," he said. "I wouldn't have put it past you to forget the whole thing. We've all been working like blacks and then you swan in without a care. Come on, we'd better get all this food down to *Woodwind*. You take the cake."

Rose suggested using the wheelbarrow for the least delicate foods, and they trundled this down the rutted path a couple of times with great success. Edna then joined them, and bore a small platter of vol-au-vents, tripping daintily in her heels, careful not to soil her mauve dress, trimmed for the occasion with an artificial orchid. At last, it was all stowed and they purred away on *Woodwind* to anchor off the old Indian reserve. Alan's boat arrived almost at the same moment, his mother and Pomfrets aboard.

Both boats tied up at the old wharf, ships lanterns were lit, though it was not yet dark, the smorgasbord was beautifully laid out. Despite the logging strike, the usual, faint summer smoke hung wispily around the Olympics, making a frilly pink sunset even pinker, while edging it with a delicate brown.

Now the guests were beginning to arrive, most by boat, some in cars, which came as near down the overgrown track as possible. One by one they hurried to wish Tim a happy birthday and add their offerings to his altar. Sophie had begun by presenting a slim blue volume, the poems of Gerard Manley Hopkins. He wished her, in return, a happy courtship and wedded bliss. "You do look quite lovely, my dear. And so does your mother."

In fact, Caroline was looking rather worn, having only just managed to complete the day's chores in time. She wore a strikingly simple dress of shantung silk, a pre-war treasure which matched her hair, and a long chain of carved amber beads which ended in a silken tassel. She handed Tim one of her Chinese horses, wrapped in a piece of embroidered silk. Edna stared her pale blue stare, Sophie, who had known nothing of this sacrifice, exclaimed, and then smiled at Alan and nodded her head as if she suddenly understood one of the more complex poems from Tim's book. Alan then kissed Sophie's hand and presented her with a rosebud corsage, which he had, for several minutes since extracting it from the icebox, been awkwardly holding behind his back. He pinned it on her white linen dress and stood back to admire her.

"You've been studying my technique," said Tim accusingly. "I wouldn't have suspected you of such panache, dear boy."

"How lucky I am to be getting such a perfect daughter," said Mrs. Graham, producing and then fastening round Sophie's neck a string of freshwater pearls. "Bless you, my dear."

It was difficult for those standing around not to feel a little tearful, but fortunately the Stanway twins just then came noisily aboard, shouting to one another that now Sophie was engaged, they need have no hesitation in kissing her. This they did, in the nick of time before the Mallows, who were following them, took Sophie's attention from everything except the puppy they were carrying for her. She could do little, from then on, except plant kisses on Simple's furrowed brow, so that even Alan grew fretful.

Tim put on a record, drinks were handed round, toasts were less and less decorously proposed as the perilous fruit punch began to affect everyone. Rose's wonderful food was first admired and then greedily consumed. The guests sat over every inch of deck, watching the sentimental moon — so well suited to this happy occasion, as Tim kept remarking — lift up like a silver dollar upon the lavender horizon.

Tim and Caroline now discovered that they shared a peculiar habit of looking at any special view, such as this, upside down. Giggling, they stood side by side by the railing, inverting themselves in turn, nearly falling over. "It enhances the colours, too," Tim asserted. "Not only the form. A whole new aesthetic realm begins to open once you look at a moon and a mountain with the top of your head touching your toes."

He deftly dropped a kiss on Caroline's hair as she took her turn, and Edna came over to see what they were up to.

"Oh, no, I was always taught in art class to frame landscape with my fingers and thumb." She extended a rather shaky hand to make a circle around the moon. "Standing on your head will only give you apoplexy, specially if you're trying to eat at the same time. I suppose those dreadful surrealists do it, who Jim pretends he likes."

"How generous you are being with your moonshine tonight," joined in Mallow. "A surfeit of delight." He raised his glass first to Tim and then to the rising moon, a notch higher already over one of the further islands where a beach fire was burning red. "Hullo!" he stopped with his mouth half open on another gulp, as a grey shape, fast and smooth, slid up to join them at the wharf.

It was the police boat. Mallow looked anxiously at Tim, who gave a slight shrug.

"Anything wrong?" he called out to the constable, who stood leaning over the rail, looking friendly but a bit sheepish. The sergeant, looking anything but friendly appeared. "Are you Mr. Timothy Spens, the owner of this boat?"

"I am."

"I have a warrant to search your boat."

"Ah well, in that case, could you be a really nice chap and do it a little later? I'm entertaining friends as you can see. It's a rather special occasion, in honour of Miss Pomfret's engagement to Mr. Graham. You wouldn't want to spoil that, I'm sure."

The sergeant said nothing, but stared grimly and tapped his gun holster. Caroline and Sophie looked at each other aghast.

"Ask all these folks to go ashore and wait, if you please."

"I don't know what this nonsense is about," replied Tim, suddenly white with anger. "Be so kind as to explain what you want, and then beat it."

A taut silence seemed to last for ever. Everyone became aware suddenly of a sound, the ship's toilet flushing. Following this, Edna swam majestically up onto the deck. "I must say, Sergeant Blair, that I am most surprised at the high-handed way you are conducting yourself. You are only a newcomer to our community. All of us," — a hiccup interrupted but did not embarrass her continuing diatribe — "have lived here, thoroughly respected, for many, many years. The Reverend Stanway's presence d-demo-demonstrates that, and Mrs. Graham."

"Come on, Edna," said James uncomfortably. "He probably thinks it's his duty."

"Don't interrupt me dear. I am doing mine, and I must say. . . ."

"I want everyone's name and address," shouted Blair, who had pulled out and opened a notebook, "and proof of identity, too."

"Sophie, dear Alan, I wouldn't have had such a thing spoil your party for all the world. But perhaps everyone should go ashore, and I can find out just what's the matter. Or thought to be the matter."

And Tim handed Caroline her shawl with something of a flourish. "There is nothing whatever to worry about, I can assure you."

"That remains to be seen," muttered Blair through his teeth, as the silenced party filed down the gangway. "Hey, not so fast there!" and he leapt aboard *Woodwind* just as Tim was turning round to go.

A couple of hours later the party, reassembled, was finishing off the evening at the Ganges Yacht Club, the name of which was grander than its interior. Two huge cherry trees and a verandah made it rather gloomy by day. At night, the brown varnished panelling and too few lights cast a similar pall. But everyone was too high-spirited to be affected. They had even managed to get the constable to join them, and he, looking rather the worse for wear from his parting words with the sergeant, mopped his face and seized with delight the proffered drink.

"William!" expostulated Rose, who had helped bring him into the world. "Just wait till I tell your mother. How could you let him do it? It nearly spoiled everything."

"I knew it would be okay, Miss Noon, really I did. But, boy, was I embarrassed! New brooms sweep clean, that's what they say. He's bound and determined to make himself a name. But, to tell the truth, Miss Noon, there has been a lot of talk about Mr. Spens and all his goings on. Now everything is swept clean, though."

"Or at least under the carpet," interrupted Mallow.

"That new broom of yours," added Tim, who was still paler than usual, "is going to change his metaphor if he doesn't look out. If he goes on with what looks like a private vendetta against me, I shall certainly sue him."

"Well, Mr. Spens, there has been word of certain individuals making moonshine. I knew you weren't, but he wouldn't believe me, being so new here. It was just as well you had the right number of legal receipts and so on."

"But even after I produced them, he insisted on taking the boat apart."

"Yes, well, yes, I'm sure you know more about that than I do, and yes, indeed, I won't say no to a drink."

Rose rescued William, and took him off to talk with Sophie. While Alan wound up the gramophone, she was pausing a moment in her never-ending dance to have a word with a sleepy Simple, curled up on one of the wicker chairs.

"Now, Skipper," said Caroline, "tell us what it was really all about."

"I'll tell you," broke in Edna, sounding triumphant, looking like a Persian cat who has successfully eaten the last drop of thick cream.

"Edna, my dear, do you not think we should be getting home?" said James, peering at her anxiously. "She's not used to so much excitement, you know. Or drink, come to that."

"Tell us, Edna," said Tim, staring at her.

"It was me that saved you, and I hope you're truly grateful. It was providential that I happened to be down in the kick-pot — pitcock — cockpit, I mean, when the police boat came. I knew at once what to do and I did it."

"And what exactly did you do?"

"I — er — disposed of all those liquor books, that's what I did. And saved you from a long spell in prison, though it wouldn't have done you any harm."

"She put them down the lavatory!" exclaimed Caroline, after a pause for thought. "I wondered why you flushed it just then, it seemed a curiously ill-chosen moment."

Tim only groaned.

"Edna, you perfect ass!" said Mallow. "Now what are we all going to do for a drink? He would never have been put in prison for having a few friends' liquor permits on board. We could have said he was looking after them for us."

"That's true," said James, looking meditative. "Is it possible, after all, that you have been getting involved in making hooch, Tim? Because if so, there won't be any more parties like this one."

"My dear fellow," returned Tim in a lofty tone, "whatever the nonsense I've committed during a misspent life, I've never given a friend anything but the real thing to drink. I may, upon occasions, have deviated from the paths of rectitude, but from now on I'm going absolutely straight." He smiled a twisted smile in Caroline's direction. "I sold out my distillery shares weeks ago. Intuition and oncoming virtue put me wise."

"But what about our permits?" urged Mallow. "Christmas is coming and New Year. We can't get any more till January."

"I fear you may well be right. But Edna did save us some tedious enquiries — thank you, Edna — and perhaps we should be grateful. Don't worry unduly. I still have friends, we can get hold of a few bottles, and I guarantee it will all be just what the label says."

"I'm delighted that you are beginning to recognise what I have done for you all," snapped Edna. "And as for this tainted stuff we've been pouring down our throats for so long — no wonder it makes some of us feel a little faint. Mouseykins, not another drop shall pass your lips."

Tim winked at James, who was pinkly blushing, while the rest started a scurry of words and toasts to hide his shame.

"Here's to the narrow way, Tim, and may it lead you straight to happiness," said Rose.

"Thank you, my dear. There's always the nylon racket next. Just think how popular that would make me with my friends. Nice pair of stockings, lady? But what will really make me popular, what had already reformed me and promises my whole life's happiness — ladies and gents, I have another announcement to add to the one we have been celebrating, however rudely interrupted, tonight." He drew Caroline's arm through his. "Wonderful, wonderful Caroline has agreed to marry me."

Chapter 16

THE REMAINDER OF THE SUMMER flashed by. The island was descending into autumn mist enlivened principally by the thought of the forthcoming Pomfret nuptials.

"It seems a waste of all those lovely big cones," remarked Caroline during this period, referring to their aged, imported pine tree. "I shall paint their tips scarlet or gold, and take samples to Victoria to that little novelty firm."

"Silly parent," jeered Sophie. "Haven't you got enough to do?"

But a bag was packed with these enticing Christmas ornaments, ready for next morning's ferry. The heavy ticking of the alarm clock primed to go off at six kept Sophie awake for much of the night. It sounded as if it had high blood pressure, and when she thought of all they had to do before Alan picked them up in his boat on the way to work and deposited them at Fulford Wharf, she was inclined to feel she had it too. When it started its raucous explosion, she silenced it at once, put on a dressing gown and slippers, and crept down to the kitchen, to fill the kettle and lay the table for her and a tray for Caroline. Then she went into the living room, smelling of bowls of dried rose petals — packets of which were also being carried to Victoria to see if there was a market for them. She wondered if the Olympics were yet on view. They reared up, strong and bold in the faint light, their kirtles of snow shrunken up to their waists. The happiness inside Sophie felt like a golden froth which the sunrise was making visible.

She returned to the kitchen singing a small, wordless song in the same sort of voice as the kettle. She wanted to give Alan a present, and began to rack her brains. For never had an engaged pair been such assiduous gift-givers: painted boxes, a long, ivory cigarette holder, pewter spirit measure, books, records, a plaster spaniel, lavender bags, gold earrings of little, tinkling bells, knitted, lumpy socks. Many of these had been filched from the house, but Sophie felt sure that Aunt Mary would perfectly understand. And she resorted to this only when all her money from cutting cascara bark had gone. She took the tray upstairs, thinking what a way it was to Caroline's bedroom, where she still slept in the big bed. Every window was wide open, uncurtained, full of sea, sky, and latticed red branches.

"Oh darling, you shouldn't have," yawned Caroline, reaching out gratefully for tea. "Don't rush away, I wanted to show you this ad." She gave Sophie an old newspaper saying that the new owners of Green Lawns Guest House in Victoria would be 'at home' on that very afternoon, happy to receive friends at the house-warming ceremony of what would henceforth be known as 'Ye Olde Green Lawns'.

"We should go and see the place in case we ever need somewhere to stay." Caroline avoided Sophie's eye.

"You mean that tea will be served — a free tea. Nuts, Mother." She hastened downstairs, gulped her breakfast and went to tend the chickens. Fungus, the new kitten, was put outside with a large bowl of milk. Caroline milked Moscow, and scalded the equipment. Simple had gone, the previous day, to stay with Moya.

By the time Alan came in to the landing stage, Sophie was there.

"I wish you'd let me take you right across, Petal," he said. "We'd get there at the same time as the ferry, and I could help you onto the bus."

"Mother is counting on us getting a ride in a car all the way. She's sure that if we travel by ferry, we'll meet someone we know."

Then Caroline arrived, carrying her case of samples and panting.

"Oh boy, what a morning!" she cried, and patted Alan's head as he helped her into the boat.

It was indeed a heavenly morning, the trail of the boat like fragile spun glass, yellows and faint pinks cloaking every island fruit tree. They passed Alan's place, then the Noons', the old Indian reserve, and the white hulls which gave Fulford Harbour such a look of holiday. The buoy which marked the channel was crowded with sleepy cormorants, reluctant to rise as they passed close by. The churning of the ferry could now be heard coming in, and they raced it up the inlet. Caroline, sitting in the bows, could also, now and then be heard singing by Sophie, who said, "She likes the verse about the rich man in his castle, the poor man at his gate."

Alan tied up deftly alongside a fish boat which they climbed across, then he walked with them carrying the suitcase, past the line of cars waiting to board the approaching ferry. "You going to town?" he enquired of the owner of a big black LaSalle.

"Why yes, Mister. You wanna ride?" The driver leant back and hospitably opened the door.

"These ladies would appreciate one."

They climbed in, and for the tenth time Alan implored Sophie to take care, and reminded her that he would be waiting to meet them that night. She waved at him frantically as they drove up the ramp, and their driver, puffing at a cigar, smiled benignly.

"You could be a couple of British war brides, I guess. How about a snifter?"

They politely declined the proffered flask, and Caroline explained their relationship.

"Well, I never would have guessed," he said with roguish gallantry. "But I certainly do pity them poor brides who came to settle on the Prairies. How do you like our coast?"

"It's wonderful," said Caroline rather absent-mindedly, before they all got out to lean on the rail as the ferry crossed back to Vancouver Island. She and Sophie really had to plan their day. It was vital to make some extra money if they did not choose to be married in rags, or accept unsuitable financial advances from Tim and Alan.

The ride into Victoria was always a pleasant one. They passed an inlet with anchored boats, water meadows of a sort, where a fine herd of jerseys grazed, a number of berry farms with loganberry vines trained along wire fences, and where, in season, cherries were massed in roadside stalls and you helped yourself and left the money in a milk bottle. Then they passed the agricultural experimental farm — a neater oasis among what were becoming motley small buildings and chicken farms. They climbed to a wonderful panorama of ocean, Gulf Islands, and the perfect ice cream cone of Mount Baker, and skirted a duck farm which resembled a snowfall of ducks, with guano advertised at a dollar a sack.

Then they passed the great Air Force base, deserted now except for a corner used by the TCA planes. They came to a sign for 'Devonshire teas' near a lake, an archery club, and a man stretched taut, hauling stump roots from a partly cleared field.

Boys raised aggressive thumbs in the hitchhike sign, and Caroline was prompted, as they passed the glimpsed observatory dome, to tell their friend how truly grateful they were for this marvelous lift.

"No problem," he answered. "A real pleasure to have you aboard. That's the finest funeral park in BC just there. They let the coffins down right nicely through a whole mess of fir branches, so you don't see the grave at all."

The hoardings increased as they entered the city, with its skirts of fretwork wooden houses, unpainted, tired, all cupolas and bow windows, towers and tiny battlements.

"That's our native gingerbread architecture," he remarked, and when Caroline murmured that the advertising hoardings should be made illegal, he seemed quite surprised, countering that they gave the place a modern air. It took a little time to convince him that they could not lunch together, and with many thanks they hastened off, anxious to finish their errands. They hastened under charming flower baskets glowing with late plantings, which bedecked each lamp standard, and shouted to each other in the excitement of the city bustle, trying to make themselves heard above the crash of the street cars. A siren 'Whoeeee', and all the traffic stopped as the fire engine, its crew still doing up buttons, streaked over the intersection.

American tourists were everywhere, buying British goods, Irish linens, tweeds, woolens, Spode or Wedgewood china, antiques. But most of the shops selling these now opened only a few days a week, because they could not get their supplies. For a moment, Caroline wondered whether she might not make a living as a negotiator between the two countries.

They walked past the extraordinary, French-derived architecture of the CPR's Empress Hotel, its mighty, creeper-clad front and penthouse skyline rearing up from what had not long ago been a swamp where Indians had landed their canoes. And now Indian totem poles stood admirably grouped on a corner lot of green lawn, their planes of sombre colour deeply carved, strong and serious, against the background of evergreens. Beyond them lay the park with its trimmed rose gardens, quintessentially English, ponds seething with ducks and swans, lily pools, herbaceous borders, a bandstand shaded by oak trees, and a cage containing a melancholy white bear. Beyond, once more, were playing fields, and a distant, glassed-in shelter on the hill by the flagpole with its speck of Union Jack feebly fluttering.

There was no time to take that walk today, but the Pomfrets did pause for a moment with their backs to the Empress Hotel to stare across the tram lines at the Princess boats in the Basin. Caroline liked to pause, too, at the War Memorial which stood on lawns sloping up to the massive, proud bulk of Parliament Buildings. It was an effigy of an infantryman loaded with battle equipment. Each time she thought, 'They shall not grow old as we grow old.'

At the souvenir shop, a number of American tourists, defeated by the closure of more expensive shops, were desperately buying nasty pennants, fake totem poles, painted shells. Caroline began to unpack her wares, and Sophie, murmuring that she would come back, hurried off to a second hand book shop where she hoped to find a present for Alan, a book by Henry Williamson she felt sure he had not read but would enjoy.

By great good luck, she almost at once came across an excellent copy of *The Pathway*, for which she handed over the rather large sum of fifty cents. She did not dare stop longer in case her mother had already been asked to leave the souvenir shop, but at least she stopped at the red traffic light, which Caroline, more impatient, always ignored. Sophie still remembered, with embarrassment, how they had once been ignominiously ordered back to the curb by a furious policeman, convincingly dressed as a London bobby.

Caroline met her with a beaming smile. She had been given a preliminary order, to be followed up in three weeks, for three hundred pine cones at five cents each. "We'll have lunch on the strength of that."

"But will there be enough cones?"

"Of course. And if there aren't, we'll go and find some in other people's gardens."

They had their lunch at the counter of the ten cent store, where the food was good and cheap, though the service was slow. After that they bought a box of chocolates for Edna and a bottle of hand lotion for Rose. They wandered vaguely among half an acre of cellophane glitter, with painted tin, glass, pulp and plastic laid out in neat and numbered allotments. Caroline managed to get hold of an assistant who directed them to a pleasant store not far away which catered for wedding garments and would be most useful later.

Just now, they could only buy what could be fitted into the empty suitcases, and then carried back to the bus terminal. However, they pushed a bassinet-like basket on wheels around, just for the fun of it, and bought a tin of cigarette tobacco for James when they found they were passing a counter displaying such things.

Soon there was only time to snatch that city treat of ice cream, tea and buns before they trudged back, heavy laden, to the depot, just in time for the bus to the ferry. Already Sophie felt she had been away for an age.

She could not wait to get back to see Alan and give him his book. "What did you buy for Tim?" she demanded.

Caroline looked slightly self-conscious. "I got a new coffee percolator. I know we'll be needing that."

Chapter 17

"WELL, THERE WAS THE LAVENDER, the fruit crop, the mushrooms, and now the pine cones. Then there's the holly, which will take us to Christmas," stated Caroline, looking up from her well-organized account book. "Weddings certainly do cost money. It's a real blow that we didn't ship that last lot of cascara bark before the price dropped."

"It wasn't exactly our fault. And I don't suppose it makes much difference in the long run."

"Luckily we only have to think of the short run. I suppose you will want to wear a sweetheart neckline and carry a splendid bouquet of mixed carnations and baby's breath, which you will hurl from the top of the stairs to a pack of bridesmaids below. Alan will wear a tuxedo. The church will be tastefully decorated with 'mums. You will finally be whirled away in a car adorned with white satin reins, the horn going full blast as if you were in an ambulance."

They both giggled at this picture, culled from the society pages of *The Daily Colonist*. But Sophie then stiffened slightly, "Mum, I am going to be a traditional white satin bride trimmed with the family lace veil which you were thanking God only the other day you hadn't lost. And carrying white lilies. But Alan will wear a dark suit, however the church is decorated."

"You can't persuade him to buy, or even rent, a morning coat?"

"No, I'm not going to try. We've been over all this before."

"I don't see why he can't wear his uniform just for once. He would look magnificent, tell him."

"That's out, too."

Caroline sighed. "Then it really would be better for you to wear an afternoon dress and a hat. Otherwise, you will look a ridiculously ill-assorted pair."

But Sophie was adamant. It was her wedding, her Canada, and she would do as the Canadians, and have a white wedding with the bridegroom in a lounge suit. But she did think her mother would look super in "sharkskin" and wearing a striking corsage. It was right and proper that James seemed delighted to give her away, he felt so like family.

"Alan's only just told me," she said, moving on to a more immediately interesting topic, "what he's giving me as a wedding present."

"What, my darling?"

"You won't believe it, Mum. A boat! Clinker built, fourteen foot, wide in the beam, an inboard Briggs and Stratton engine, partly decked-in and copper-fastened. The sort of boat we'll be able to squeeze all the Cubs into, for island jaunts."

"Cubs! How ever many are you planning to have?"

"Little Scouts, you idiot, not children! Alan was a Sea Scout, you know, and I've decided I can take the Cub pack over when I have the car down at the yard. You were the person who first suggested it."

"Well, it won't be the right time of year to go honey-mooning in it, perfect as that might seem for spring."

"No, we really do want to go to Vancouver. Then we can spend some time with Alan's mother, as well as going up to the snow."

"And when you get back I shall go off to Mexico. Just as long as the house is occupied by one or the other of us, I suppose it will be alright by Aunt Mary. I'll come back when the rains stop, and you and Alan can happily depart to your island and live on wiener roasts."

"Mum, seriously, do you really want to marry Tim? I keep wondering if you're doing it as a sort of last-ditch measure."

"Well, it's the only way of getting my Chinese horse back. It's nice that you will have your own boat. Perhaps I can hope for a small car. Even a used one. For that, I will gladly give Tim the second China horse. "

"Would Daddy have liked him?" Sophie's face went very pink as she managed to ask that question which had been plaguing her.

"I believe he would have given his consent, everything considered," Caroline answered thoughtfully. "He'd know how much I deserve a holiday, and some loving care."

"Don't be flippant. Do you love Tim?"

"In my own way, I do. I am middle-aged, Sophie, you can't expect quite the same transports which sweep you and Alan off your feet."

For a dreadful moment, while Sophie stared at her mother, she was prey to fearful pictures of her and Tim enjoying connubial bliss, but these were almost at once discarded in favour of others more platonic. She was confused again, but only for a moment.

"My God!" she cried, "You're not contemplating a double wedding, by any chance? I've been wondering why you haven't announced any plans, but I kept quiet just in case you were having second thoughts about it all."

"What a brilliant idea. Mother is forced to console her daughter's discarded lover. All four are reconciled in a ceremony of generation-spanning loveliness!"

"Mum!"

"Don't worry, Sophie, I never thought of such a thing. If Tim and I really do get married — perhaps it would be better if you would simply allow us to live in sin — it will be in a very staid and decent ceremony, not a bouquet in sight. After you and Alan come back from your honeymoon, so that Alan can give me away. It's the least he can do, after all I've given him."

"Jeepers! What would Aunt Mary say!"

Sophie stared at Caroline, aghast, and then began to laugh. They sat across the table from one another, the account books between them, and both laughed — louder and louder.

Glossary of Terms

Ambrosical: Typical of Ambrose (Mallow); also his wife's cooking.

Batching: A man living on his own.

Cascara bark: Collected and sold for its laxative properties. A good way to make a little extra pin money.

Cesar Franck: 19th century Belgian-French organist and composer known for his romantic and expansive style.

Combinations: English term for long woolen underwear — for men or women — often known in the rest of Canada as "Stanfield's."

Cos lettuce: The English name for romaine lettuce.

Cowichan sweater: thick, raw wool sweaters knitted by the Indians of the Cowichan (Khowitzan) Valley on Vancouver island. The sweaters were famous for their local native designs in brown and their ideal insulating qualities in the damp West Coast climate. They were so popular they were one of the symbols of life on the West Coast of British Columbia.

Cretonne: Sturdy, unglazed cotton cloth with pattern printed on one or both sides; used for slip covers or curtains, etc.

Doukhobors: Groups of immigrants who took refuge in Saskatchewan in the late 1800s, fleeing persecution in Russia for their unorthodox religious beliefs. By the 1920s, there were about ninety Doukhobor, or "spirit wrestler," communes in BC, particularly in the Castlegar area. Referred to here are the

"Freedomites," a radical sect, not to be confused with the peaceful main Doukhobor community.

Fichu: A small, triangular scarf often frilled with lace.

Kedgeree: East Indian dish popular with English people. It consisted largely of brown rice, smoked fish and hard boiled eggs, with mango chutney.

Kirtle: Gown or outer petticoat.

Liquor permit: A permit allowing individuals to purchase specified amounts of alcoholic beverages from provincial government liquor stores. The system was essentially an attempt to ration public consumption following the ending of prohibition and the starting of government-run liquor stores (pioneered by British Columbia in the 1930s). The liquor permit system was in use throughout Canada, except Quebec, which was more liberal. Permits were cheap, (e.g. about 50 cents a year in Alberta, $1.00 year in Manitoba). In Manitoba, a permit allowed purchase of one 26-ounce bottle of spirits per month, two 26-ounce bottles of wine per week, and 24 pints of beer per day. British Columbia's system was much the same. The liquor permit system was abolished in 1947.

Marocain: A dress fabric made of silk, or other material.

Mousetrap: Strong cheddar cheese (good for a mousetrap).

Musquash: A muskrat fur; very durable. The "rat" was replaced euphemistically.

Palliasse: From the French *paillasse.* A straw mattress.

Pram: In the nautical sense, a British term for a skiff or dinghy.

Puce: Flea-coloured; that is purple and brown.

Remittance man: Found frequently in the colonies, a man paid by his family to live abroad, and leave them and England alone.

Sea cows: Although the dugong is also known as a sea cow, the reference here is to Stellar's Sea Cow, a related animal. In the public mind at this time Stellar's Sea Cow was famous for becoming extinct, like the Dodo and the Great Auk. Stellar's Sea Cows were huge, docile animals living along the Pacific shores of Alaska. They moved in herds and had a habit of schooling up in support of a wounded member, making massed slaughter easy by Russian sailors hunting for food. Sea cows had disappeared by the end of the eighteenth century.

Sprigged: An ornamental branch design featuring small shoots or "sprigs," used on muslin, cotton, and other fabrics.

Tippet: A fur cape or muffler.

Topi: Anglo-Indian word for a pith helmet.

Weepers: Whiskers so abundant they droop like a weeping willow.

Wrack: Seaweed and wood cast up by the ocean. Here, used for garden fertilizer.